Amélie Rives

Virginia of Virginia

Amélie Rives

Virginia of Virginia

ISBN/EAN: 9783743367630

Manufactured in Europe, USA, Canada, Australia, Japa

Cover: Foto ©ninafisch / pixelio.de

Manufactured and distributed by brebook publishing software (www.brebook.com)

Amélie Rives

Virginia of Virginia

"I—I—I LOOK A AWFUL FOOL—DON'T I?"—*page* 125.

VIRGINIA OF VIRGINIA

A Story

BY

AMÉLIE RIVES

AUTHOR OF
"A BROTHER TO DRAGONS, AND OTHER OLD-TIME TALES" ETC.

ILLUSTRATED

NEW YORK
HARPER & BROTHERS, FRANKLIN SQUARE
1888

Copyright, 1888, by HARPER & BROTHERS.

All rights reserved.

ILLUSTRATIONS.

	PAGE
"I—I—I LOOK A AWFUL FOOL—DON'T I?" *Frontispiece*	
"I CAN'T COME TO DINNER"	11
"AW-W-W POPO!"	43
ON THE TOP OF PETER'S MOUNTAIN	65
"I GWINE TAKE DAT DAR OUTLANDISH THING OFFEN YO', HONEY"	139
"HE MUST 'A' HAD A MIGHTY LEETLE CROP"	161

VIRGINIA OF VIRGINIA.

I.

"IT'S a girl," said Roden, laying a wager with himself. "No; it's a boy. Hanged if it isn't a girl!" He took his short brier-wood pipe from his mouth, knocked out its contents against the side of the wagon, and pocketed it.

The time of the year was January, the scene a country road in Virginia, and it was drizzling, a thick Scotch drizzle, abetted by a lusty east wind. Even the branches of the straggling locust-trees that lined the red road seemed clogged with it. It hung in folds upon the sides of the mountains, and was blown in masses between the clefts of the rolling meadows.

Roden was not only a new arrival in Virginia, but in America, and the impression made upon him had not, to speak very moderately, been favorable. Coming from Washington, some one in the train had asked him if it did not remind him of England. He had answered with some curtness that it did not, demanding at the same time why he should be particularly reminded of England by the state of the weather in Virginia. His interlocutor had replied with the never-failing urbanity of the Virginian farmer, that "anybody could tell he was an Englisher by th' way he talked, and them loose pants."

At the moment he first saw the figure alluded to, the owner of the British accent and the "loose pants" was shivering in spite of the top-coat turned up about his ears and the soft hat pulled down to meet it.

It was indeed a girl; she wore a soft hat, the counterpart of his own, fashioned of the same stuff as her dark-gray jacket and the kirtle which reached just below her knees. On her legs were shooting-gaiters of russet leather, decidedly influenced as to color by the tyrannic soil, and on her feet stout cowhide boots. She carried a gun on her shoulder, and a game-bag hung at her side. She further appeared to be bounded on the east, west, north, and south by dogs. An old mastiff lounged sulkily at her heels. Far in front, a collie gave chase to a stately buzzard, which sailed away undisturbed by its pursuer's shrill barking, while an asthmatic pug sought a Juggernautal fate between the ponderous wagon-wheels, and a little black-and-tan terrier, sniffing hither and thither among the mist-drenched weeds, reminded Roden of the accounts of certain mammoth ants as related by the credulous Herodotus.

The girl, who had been walking with head bent, looked up as the creaking of the wagon-wheels arrested her attention.

"I beg your pardon," said Roden, "but can you tell me if I am on the right road to Caryston Hall? I think that's the name."

She looked at him seriously for a moment, and then said, "Yes, you are. I s'pose you're th' new Englishman. Are you?"

"I suppose so," said Roden. "My name is Roden. I have bought a farm somewhere in this neighborhood, and it is called Caryston Hall."

"That's it," she said; "you're right. My father's th' overseer there. Why don't you get down and walk? You look so cold. I'll show you."

"Thank you," said Roden; "I think I will;" and he jumped down beside her.

Judging by her attire, he had at first thought her a sporting country-woman of his own, like himself an exile in a far country; but after she had spoken he found that the soft, slow intonation was strange to his ear. "The overseer business explains it," he thought. "She is a native, and this language is Virginian." In the mean time the girl was also making mental observations. He was the third English gentleman she had seen, though of immigrant Britishers she had known full threescore and ten. She was thinking that he had spoken to her with an unusual civility, and wondering how long it would continue. Civility this young Virginian had not found to be a characteristic of the British settler in her native State.

"I'm very lucky to have met you," said Roden, as they walked on, having dismissed the services of the ancient wagoner, whom the girl addressed as "Unc' Dick." "I would like to ask you some questions about the place, and it's awfully kind of you to go back with me."

She said, indifferently, and without lifting her eyes this time, "Oh, I was goin' back anyway! 'Tisn't any bother."

Her long strides matched Roden's exactly, and the rapid motion through the stiffly yielding medium under foot began to warm his veins. They saw the serpentine flourish of Unc' Dick's voluminous whip-lash outlined against the pale sky as the wagon descended a hill just in front of them. Two more buzzards appeared, slanting in still absorption towards the west. Instantly the collie was after them.

"Why didn't you telegraph?" said the girl, suddenly.

"I did," said Roden, with some grimness. "I telegraphed twice. I also had the pleasure of rereading both telegrams when I arrived at the station about an hour ago."

"Seems to me," she said, turning to look over her shoulder at the mastiff, pug, and terrier, that were having a tow-row over an old shoe (which same seem to be sown in lieu of corn in the thorns by the Virginian way-side)—"Seems to me that letters reach us twice as quick as telegrams, anyhow.

You must have thought it funny we didn't send for you?"

"I don't know that I found it very amusing," said Roden, truthfully, adding, in a tone of helpless aggravation, "All my luggage was left behind in Washington."

At this direct appeal the overseer's daughter at first looked as sorrowful as even Roden could have desired, bursting the next moment into peals and roulades of laughter. Roden, after the first sharp inclination to feel angry, joined in her mirth.

"Pore feller!" she said at last, taking off her rain-soaked hat, on which she appeared to dry her brimming eyes — " Pore feller! it all seems awful to you out here, don't it?"

"It does," said Roden in his heart, but out loud he replied with mendacious civility that it did not. He was, moreover, occupied in a close scrutiny of her uncovered locks. They were of a pale golden color, lying close to her forehead in thick, round rings, after the manner of a child's, and clustering heavily, with the dampness. As he stood beside her he saw also that she was very tall, taller than most tall women, and that her fair throat, rising boy-like from a dark-red kerchief, had unusual suggestions of muscle beneath its smooth surface.

Presently they walked on. The top of a tolerably high hill was soon reached, surmounted, as Roden at first thought, by an almost impenetrable thicket. As they approached nearer, however, he perceived an aperture in the mass of foliage, and a long wooden gate, hanging by one hinge in an aimless, desultory manner, and ornamented also as to its dingy gray with copious splashes of red mud. On either post were rusty iron vases, wherefrom there sprouted two stunted specimens of the aloe tribe. One of these vases, having been broken some years before, hung over to one side with a suggestion of inanimate sentimentality highly ludicrous. Some kind Samaritan had thrust a stick in between its disabled joints, thus preventing it from utter downfall.

The view beyond the gate was unique, and to Roden rather pleasant after his morning's experience. The lawn proper was shaped like a lady's slipper, and outlined by a gravel carriage-drive. It seemed as though some Titaness might have set a careless foot among the surrounding shrubbery, crushing out of existence all save a bordering fringe of evergreen and acacias. The long, low house of red brick —with wings out-spread after a protective, hen-like fashion in the direction of the many out-houses—was to be seen through the bare branches of two splendid tulip-trees. A little Alderney heifer was grazing near the portico, and some dorkings stood resignedly on long yellow legs under the shelter of the large box-bushes.

As they worked along the sinuous carriage-way Roden looked with a feeling of ownership at the glimpses of distant hill and forest, as visible through the crowding tree-stems. Here he was to make his home for at least the next two years, and he was glad not to find it so bad as he had expected.

As she opened the hall door the girl said to him, "Father won't be here until six o'clock. I'll have you some dinner ef you want it. But you'd better go to your room first, hadn't you, you're so wet?— I'll send you some things the larst Englishman left behind him. There's a barth ready, and plenty of towels. I'm used to fixin' for you English, you see. Well, good-by till you're dressed; then I'll show you over the house."

She sent a little "nigger," who conducted him with wordless dignity to the apartment allotted him, and who some five minutes later returned again with the "last Englishman's things." That personage must have been of very slight proportions

"I CAN'T COME TO DINNER."

UNIV. OF
CALIFORNIA

and medium height, whereas Roden stood six foot one in his stockings, and was of excellent figure. He struggled for some time with the meagre garments, and then decided that he could not put in an appearance until his own garments should be dry. At this moment some one knocked at the door with the announcement — " Dinner rade-y."

"I can't come to dinner," said Roden at the key-hole. "The clothes won't fit me. Say I am very sorry."

The departing footsteps echoed down the narrow corridor that led to the room which had been given him, and Roden, who had taken the silk coverlet from the bed and rolled himself in it, stretched out before the fire of pine cones in the big fireplace. The room was large and square, and had hangings of faded green silk embroidered with tarnished gold. A ponderous mahogany wardrobe, looking like nothing so much as a grim wooden mausoleum, occupied nearly all of one wall. Facing this on the opposite side of the room was a low chest of drawers, also of mahogany, with brass lion-head handles. A square mirror in a wrought-brass frame hung over it. The bedstead was low and wide, with foot-board and head-board of a like height. Voluminous curtains of faded green fell from a mahogany frame fastened to the ceiling, and were tucked back behind brass knobs on either side of the bed. There was a huge pale-green paper screen crowded into one corner of the room, and behind this Roden discovered a bath-tub and a washhand-stand. One picture hung over the mantle-shelf, a reproduction of the Madonna of the Chair, done evidently with a very hard and very pointed lead-pencil, and faintly tinted with pink chalk as to lips and cheeks.

Roden lay in the soft embrace of his one Indian-like garment and stared up at this work of art. He became fascinated in wondering how many days it must have taken its indefatigable perpetrator to make the million of little scratches that composed it. He wondered if it were the production of generations past or present. Could Virginia herself have been guilty of it? He thought not. At all events he hoped not. Her voice seemed to put her beyond the pale of such possibilities. He recalled it to his memory's ear now, with a distinct sensation of pleasure. There had been in it a certain rich sonorousness. It was grave, serious, soft as the rush of the rain through the short grass without. A beautiful voice attracts men always, even as the *timbre* of a fine instrument invariably attracts a musician. It is, so to speak, the overture to the whole character. No; the pink-cheeked Virgin, with the slate-colored infant tilted against her wooden and unresponsive bosom, could never have been the work of the maiden in the Rosalind costume. Never, never! Why, now that he thought of it, should the cheeks of the pictured Madonna so blush? unless, perhaps, at the culpable drawing of her sacred proportions. Why should she have been drawn at all? There was absolutely no reason that he could discover. The pine cones crackled and blazed up with a savory smell. The fragrant warmth stole pleasantly over the young fellow's relaxed limbs. The pink-and-gray Madonna faded slowly and surely away in a golden haze. There was a pleasant humming as of a summer field within his ears. Why did he seem to be pulling up a scarlet window-blind, which obstinately refused to remain in position, in order to let three large black sheep gambol at their pleasure about that imposing mahogany catafalque? And why did the loss of a brass key at least three feet long, and which seemed to belong to his hat-box, occasion him such acute mortification when called upon by a very old woman in blue kid low-shoes to explain its whereabouts? And why did — and why didn't — and what on earth made them all? Roden had not slept so soundly since leaving British soil.

He was awakened by a vigorous rapping at the door. He sat up and rolled himself more tightly in the big green silk quilt.

"Who is it?" he said.

"'Tis yo' clo'es," replied a solemn voice. "An' please, sur, ter dress ez quick ez you kin, 'case supper soon be rade-y."

Roden admitted his once more dry outfit through a small aperture in the door, after having inquired as to the time, and finding that he had slept two hours.

"Miss Faginia she say ez how she ben think you'd rayther eat yo' supper jiss so, 'thout sp'ilin' it with er sorter dinner," chanted the monotonous voice without.

Roden admitted that "Miss Faginia" had been quite right in her conjecture. In half an hour he went out into the big hall, which, divided by three arches, ran through the centre of the house. Over the first was a fine moose-head. There were skins of many beasts here and there on the slippery oak floor, and straight-backed chairs set against the panelled wall, which some barbarian had painted white. A much-carved oak table on one side supported a large silver flagon and two old-fashioned tankards. On the other was an old-fashioned hat-rack, filled mostly with feminine head-gear of various makes and sizes. A pair of branchy antlers supported riding-canes of all descriptions.

Guided by the sounds of a piano softly played, Roden opened a door on his left, and found himself in a large firelit room, whose walls were absolutely covered with pictures large and small, all in old Italian frames, all more or less stiff and ill painted, all hung, regardless of size or shape, as close to one another as they could possibly be placed. The effect of the thus concentrated colors was, in spite of the defects of the pictures themselves, quaint and jewel-like. Over the mantle of carved oak reached upward to the ceiling an enormous square mirror in the style of the First Empire. On one side of the room was hung its mate, also in lonely grandeur, and facing the portrait of a very rosy dame in a still rosier tulle dress, the whole suggesting in color the presence of the all-pervading Virginian soil.

Just under this second mirror was a piano, and at this piano was standing the overseer's daughter, striking idle chords with her left hand.

She had taken off her Rosalind costume, and appeared in a blue homespun dress, neat and scant of make, and with her two big braids hanging over her shoulders.

"Oh, it's you!" she said, addressing Roden. "I was just trying th' piano to see 'f any 'v the keys 'd stuck since the last Englishman left; but th' haven't. D' you like music?" she went on, in her vibrant voice, which seemed in some strange manner to harmonize with the firelight and the now steady hum of the rain without. "I'll tell you, before you say anything, I can play very well."

Roden found her open conceit a very novel and amusing sensation, but when she had struck a few chords firmly, her long fingers sinking in among the keys as might the fingers of a miser among the gold coin that he loved, he thought no more of anything save the melody that filled the room.

"Gad!" said he, when she had ceased, "I should say you could play, rather! Where on earth—who taught you?"

"No one," she said, absently, striking noiseless chords with her left hand, and not looking at him. "I've heard people, and I do 't by ear. And the men that 've had th' Hall 've been awful kind 'bout lettin' me play—an' that's all," comprehensively—adding, with sudden irrelevance, "Were your clothes quite dry?"

"Quite," he assured her; "but they are beastly dirty to come to supper in."

"I dried them myself," she continued, taking no notice of his last assertion. "Such work as I had, too! I really think if Milly hadn't helped me, you'd 'a' been in —in—in your green silk quilt now."

She leaned forward for some moments, laughing, with her head against the music-rack, so that the piano reverberated shrilly with the clear sound. Roden laughed with her.

"Who told you—the little nigger?" he asked. "And who is Milly?"

She got suddenly to her feet, as suddenly becoming grave, and closed the piano.

"Milly's one o' th' darkies," she said. "Come and get your supper."

He followed her across the wide hall into the dining-room, and found that supper at Caryston Hall was a very pretty meal. It was served on finest but much-darned damask, by the light of six tall candles in silver candlesticks, each ornamented by a little petticoat of scarlet silk, which gave them the appearance of diminutive coryphées pirouetting on one slender wax leg. A bowl of violets and primroses occupied the centre of the table, flanked on either side by crystal dishes, filled, the one with the pale amber of honey, the other with the deep crimson of cranberries.

The overseer's daughter poured out tea behind a great silver urn, while on her right hand a monstrous cut-glass flagon foamed with richest milk. "Positively artistic," thought Roden, feeling a certain respect in his British breast for this little maiden of Virginia who could evolve out of her own country-bred brain effects so charming. "It's a beastly pity!" he told himself, though in what the pity consisted he could not quite have told any one else, unless perhaps that a being so gifted with a talent for instrumental music, and the setting forth of appetizing supper-tables, should be hemmed in from further progress by the scarlet soil of her native State, and should murder his sovereign's language with ruthless regularity by beheading some words and cutting the remainder in two.

He also pondered somewhat as to the way in which Virginian overseers and their children expected to be treated by resident foreigners. He noticed that the girl ate nothing herself, sitting with her hand in her lap after she had poured out his cup of tea, and pulling idly at the frayed edge of the table-cloth, with eyes downcast. He wished very much that he knew how to address her, and was casting about in his mind as to how he might find out her surname without being rude, when she answered him directly.

"My name is Virginia"—she said "Faginia"—but it came softly to the ear—"Virginia Herrick."

"They ought to have called you 'Julia,'

Miss Herrick," said the young Englishman, gravely regarding her grave face.

"Why?" she said, with her swift change from listless to alert—"why ought they? It's a hijeous name, I think."

"It isn't very pretty—not near so pretty as 'Faginia,'" said Roden, gallantly; "but there was a fellow once called Herrick who was always writing songs to 'Julia.'"

"Oh," said the girl, with a sudden dawning in her sombre eyes, "that's the man wrote 'To Daffodils' and 'Primroses' and things, ain't it?"

"That's the man," he said.

"Well," she replied, slowly, "I don't see why *I* ought to be called Julia. Her last name wa'n't Herrick, 'cause he wouldn't 'a' written those kynder things to his sister, and a man wouldn't 'a' taken th' trouble to write songs to 's wife."

"Why?" said Roden, fixing on her his eyes, at whose blueness she began to wonder in a vague way. Thus looking out from the young man's sunburnt, weather-marked face they reminded her of some vivid, sky-colored flower springing into sudden azure among brown summer grasses.

"Why?" he repeated. "Are all Virginian husbands so ungallant to their wives?"

"So what?" she said, contracting her level brows.

"So rude, so careless of their wives."

"Oh, I reckon so," she made answer. "I don't know much 'bout men 'n' their wives. My father's died when I was born, an' somehow I don't take much to women, nor they tuh me. But I know 'nuff," she supplemented, "to know a man ain't goin' to make a fuss over 's wife."

"If you ever marry," said Roden, "do you think you will put up with that sort of thing?"

"Sho!" she exclaimed, rising and pushing back her chair, which made a sharp sound on the polished oak of the floor. "I'll never marry in *this* world."

"Well, you certainly won't in the next," said Roden, smiling broadly; "that is, if you're orthodox."

"What o'dox?" she said, pausing to question him, with one hand on the table.

"Orthodox—if you believe all that the Bible tells you."

"Well, I don't" she said, quickly; "not by a long sight. I don't believe all those things got into one place like that ark without killin' each other clean out. An' I don't believe those b'ars eat them children for laughin' at that ole feller's bal' head (I've laughed at many of 'em myself, an' no b'ars 'ain't ever eat me; an' if 'twas right then, 'twould be right now). No, I cert'n'y ain't or-or-orth'dox," said Miss Virginia Herrick, beginning to clear away the supper-dishes.

"You're not commonplace, at all events," Roden told himself, as, after having obtained her permission to smoke, he lighted a cigarette. It was now past eight o'clock, and still no signs of the recreant overseer. Roden occupied himself with putting many questions of a more business-like character to Miss Herrick, as she moved about the room restoring things to their proper places. He found that the little petticoats which ornamented the candles were some more of the things left by "the last Englishman;" and that the primroses and violets grew in what was called the "greenhouse," a narrow glass-fronted corridor reaching along the front of the east wing of the house, and opening out of the dining-room.

He said he would like to go in to look at it, and she at once conducted him there, carrying no candle, since a full-moon looked in at them through the lattice of the winter trees. A thick soft air, spongy with dampness, closed about them. The flowers rose dark and redolent on all sides. Roden could make out the large, bunchily growing leaves of a magnolia-tree outside, seen in rich relief against the dim sky.

Roden, who had an artistic soul, found

much pleasure in watching her. He was beginning to think that in her own unique way she was beautiful, and she was certainly shaped like a young caryatid.

After she had answered various queries about house and out-house, niggers and stables, they returned to the dining-room, and lifting one of the tall candlesticks from a side-table, she opened one of the many doors.

"I'm going to father's room," she announced; "'f you like you can come too. Most of 'em" (alluding probably to the preceding Englishmen)—"most of 'em liked to smoke there. I've got my spinnin' an' some things to do. Ef you want to stay here, there's books." She made a comprehensive sweep with her candleless hand in the direction of a low bookcase which ran around three sides of the room.

"I think I'll come with you, if you really don't mind," said Roden.

"Lor', no!" she hastened to assure him.

"But 'f you don't like dogs an' 'coons an' things, you'd better not."

"Oh, I don't mind 'coons and — and things," said Roden, somewhat vaguely. "I'll come, thank you."

They went down a long hall, descended a little stair-way whereon the moonlight fell bluely through a square window high above, down more steps, along another passage with sharp turns, and in at an already open door. An old negress, vividly turbaned, was heaping wood upon an already immense fire.

"Lor', mammy!" called Miss Herrick, "for mercy's sakes stop! 'F you put any more wood on that fire you'll have to get up on th' roof an' shove 't down th' chimney." The "'coons and things" were already crowding about them.

Roden recognized several of his canine friends of the morning, and there were, moreover, two splendid old hounds, which at sight of their evidently beloved "Faginia" set up a most booming yowl of welcome. There were also the 'coon; a curious flat-stomached little beast, that flew about after a startling fashion from chair to chair, and which Miss Herrick introduced as a "chipmunk;" a corn-crake; a young screech-owl; and three large Persian cats.

All these pets, he discovered later, had been presented from time to time by the "last Englishman," or "the Englishman before the last," or "the Englishman before the one with the glass eye," or the fat wife, or the ugly sister, or what not.

"If I can only add a gorilla or a condor to this unique collection," reflected Roden, "my position is assured. I will probably be forever the 'last Englishman,' and I will always be mentioned as 'the Englishman who gave me the gorilla.'"

He then sat down in a corner as far removed as was consistent with politeness from the other inhabitants of the apartment, and occupied himself with watching " Faginia," her " mammy," and the " things."

"Aunt Tishy," said Miss Herrick, indicating him with a movement of her bright head, as he sat withdrawn into his coign of vantage, like a hermit-crab within its shell, "that's the new Englishman, Mr. Roden."

"How yo' do, sur? Hope yo' coporosity segastuate fus rate, sur," quoth the dusky dame, with an elephantine dab, supposed in the innocence of her Virginian heart to correspond to the courtesy of civilization.

"My what?" said Roden.

"She means she hopes you are well," explained Virginia, about whose neck the raccoon was coiling himself with serpentine affection.

"Oh yes, thanks, very well. Are you?" said Roden.

"Gord! yes, sur; Tishy she *al'uz* well— ain' she, honey?" This last appeal to Virginia.

"Oh yes," said that young woman " 'cep'

when you get th' misery, or th' year-ache in th' middle o' th' coldest nights, an' have me huntin' all over creation for somethin' to put in your year. Oh yes!"

"G'way, chile!" exclaimed the thus maligned personage, with an air of indignant sufferance. "If I didn' know yer wuz jess projeckin', I sutny would feel bade."

"Oh no, you wouldn't," said her mistress, easily. "*This* one," again indicating Roden, "'s goin' in fur horse-racin'. Some of his horses 's comin' day after to-morrer. That's better 'n Herefordshire cattle, ain't it?"

"Co'se *you* think so," said Aunt Tishy, with something between a sniff and a grunt, as she settled herself in the chimney-corner with a basket of darning, and fell to work, stretching the stockings to be mended over a little gourd.

"Why, Aunt Tishy?" said Roden, beginning to feel as though he were a character in a book, and might spoil the plot by saying the wrong thing.

The old negress looked up at him over her big gold-rimmed spectacles, with her great underlip pushed out, showing its pale yellowish lining.

"Lor'! sur," she said, "Miss Faginny's plum crazy 'bout horses. Ev'ybody on de place 'll tell you dat. I alwuz hol's as how somebody done cunjur her mar 'fo' she was bown. Dat's why she so run made 'bout horses. Somebody sutny *is* cunjur Miss Faginny. I'll say dat with my last bref!"

"Oh, shut up, mammy!" here interpolated Virginia.

"I sutny will," reiterated the old black.

"Cert'n'y will what?" said Miss Herrick; "shut up? I'm sure I hope so, and I know Mr. Roden does."

She rose and put down the raccoon, who immediately clambered up to the carven top of an old oak press close by, and hung there, smiling genially.

Virginia busied herself in getting out her spinning-wheel and winding the distaff with blue wool. As she sat down to her spinning, with her closely plaited fair hair falling into her lap, a novel thought suggested itself to Roden, namely, that this blond maiden might be a Desdemona dressed up as Marguerite, with the Moor concealed as her nurse.

He watched with a strange sensation of unreality the whirring wooden wheel, the soft falling of the blue thread upon the floor, the dusky smoke-stained rafters of the room, wherefrom hung strings of onions and red peppers in gay festoons; the old negress, wrinkled as to her black face with busy absorption; the moving of the different creatures in the sombre depths of shadow. Now it was the glint of the corncrake's flame-like crest as he thrust an inquisitive head from his position on a shelf over the mantle. Now the white gleam of the raccoon's sharp teeth as he grinned with an amiable persistency upon the room and its inmates. Now the old hounds grumbled uneasily in their sleep, or the Persian cats leaned against his legs with luxurious, undulating appeals to be caressed.

"Why don' yo' sing, honey?" said Aunt Tishy; "yo' know yo' kyarn' harf wuk ef yo' don' sing."

"Yes, do sing, Miss Virginia," said Roden. "A nig—I mean a darky song," he added, quickly.

"What shall I sing, mammy?" questioned she.

"Dat 'pen's on whut kinder song de gen-'leman wants."

"Well, what kind do you want?" she asked him.

"Something characteristic," he replied.

Thus adjured, she sang to him, in a very rich contralto voice, the following ditty:

> "Ole ark she reel, ole ark she rock,
>   Settin' up on de mountain-top.
>   Ole ark a-movin', movin', chillun—
>   Ole ark a-movin, I thank Gord!

"Ole hyah, whut make yo' eye so pop?
　I thank Gord fuh tuh see how tuh hop!
　　Ole ark a-movin', movin', chillun—
　　Ole ark a-movin', I thank Gord!

"Ole hyah, whut make yo' legs so thin?
　I thank Gord fuh tuh split 'gin de win'!
　　Ole ark a-movin', movin, chillun—
　　Ole ark a-movin', I thank Gord!

"Ole hyah, whut make yo' hade so bal'?
　I thank Gord ben butt 'gin de wall!
　　Ole ark a-movin', movin', chillun—
　　Ole ark a-movin', I thank Gord!"

Before Roden could say anything, she rose and put aside her spinning-wheel, holding out to him her long shapely hand, which was covered with tan as with a brown glove to within about an inch of her homespun sleeve. "Good-night," she said; "I'm sleepy. Father won't be here now till tuh-morrer. I s'pec' he slept at Cyarver's. Everything's ready—your barth an' everything."

Thus dismissed, Roden took himself off

to bed. As he dropped to sleep to the tune of "Ole ark a-movin'," he was conscious of uncomfortable memories concerning haunted rooms in old Virginian mansions. Not that he believed in ghosts—Heaven forbid!—but some one might—some little nigger, you know—might play one a trick.

He was roused suddenly and unpleasantly by three solemn raps on the door at his bed's head.

"Well—what is it?" he said, in an unnecessarily loud tone.

"'Tis me—Aun' Tishy," replied an unmistakable voice. "Please come to de do', sur, jess a minute."

He answered this appeal, opening the door cautiously an inch or two, whereupon she thrust into his hands a little white bundle.

"Dis heah's fo' yo' to war tuh-night. Marse Gawge he don' war no night-shuts, and dey ain' none o' th' other Englishers lef' none; so I jess stole you one o' Miss Faginny's. Don' say nothin' 'bout it, please, sur, 'case ef dar *is* one thing Miss Faginny's 'tic'lar 'bout, 'tis her clo'es."

Roden took the long white garment gingerly, as men lift a young baby, bade Aunt Tishy good-night, and closed the door. He then went to the fire and began to examine what that colossal personage had inferred to be " Miss Faginny's night-shut."

It was a capacious arrangement of very thin linen, and superfine little frills of a like material—hardly the garment in which an overseer's daughter would have wooed repose. The young man looked at it carefully and gravely from all points of view, then went and hung it over the mirror, and returning to bed, regarded it with the mute attention which he had before bestowed on the drab-colored Madonna. It was a dainty thing, probably a relic of some previous Englishman's wife or daughter, and the rosy light from the handful of fresh cones which he had thrown on the fire stole in and out of its sheer folds caressingly.

He left it hanging there, and the last thing he remembered that night was its gleam, as of a pretty ghost in the firelit dusk of the big room.

II.

He could have sworn that he had slept but a moment when a terrific squeaking and squealing, yelping and growling, under his windows, aroused him with sufficient abruptness.

His first idea was that the " 'coons and things " were " killin' each other clean out," after the fashion of Miss Virginia's supposition in regard to the Scriptural beasts in the story of the ark.

Looking out, however, he saw that a large black and white hog was being chased, nipped, barked at, and otherwise maltreated by the mastiff and the collie. The frightened beast rushed hither and thither, squealing and grunting, and the two dogs followed, falling over each other in the eagerness of pursuit. After a while the mad trio disappeared to the farther end of the long terrace.

Dawn had just broken. The east was one deep even tone of mellow gold, translucent, palpitating. Over against it lay gray streamers as of a tattered banner. The morning-star seemed to spin with a cold blue glitter as of ice in the voluptuous saffron of its setting. A band of trees stood out against the vivid east, with bold relief of indigo leaves and branches, like a gigantic tracery of unknown hieroglyphics. Over field and lawn a white steam rose and melted slowly — blue hill and tawny meadow appearing and disappearing as the pearly masses rolled together or dissolved.

Roden heard with supreme delight the confidential voice of a little nigger announcing through the key-hole (their favorite channel of communication) that his "trunks dun come."

He got with all speed through his ablutions, and, when his boxes were brought, into a well-worn shooting-coat and knickerbockers, determining as he laced his hobnailed boots to "do" the farm thoroughly that morning, and devote the rest of the day to mountain-climbing and explorations generally.

As he went out on the square portico at the front of the house he met Miss Herrick, again in her boy's dress, leading the mastiff and the collie with either hand. She had evidently been to the rescue of the black and white hog, and both dogs had a sneaky appearance, as though they knew a flogging was in store for them.

"Mornin'," she said to Roden, with her grave directness of regard. "How'd you sleep?"

Before he could reply, a voice, rising in long, wailing tones upon the chill air, interrupted them.

"O-o-o-o Po!" it called; "O-o-o-o *Po!*" then a pause as if waiting for a reply. Then again, "Aw-w-w Po-po! Aw-w-w *Po*-po!"

"It's father callin' Popo," explained Virginia.

"Who's Popo? Another nigger?"

"Yes," briefly.

"What does 'Popo' stand for? Napoleon?" questioned Roden, much interested.

"No," she said. "'F you wait an' listen you'll hear. Father always calls like that at first. 'F Po answers tuhecly he'll jus' stop. 'F he don't answer, father'll jus' go on callin' till he says th' whole name."

"AW-W-W POPO!"

Roden listened with absorbed attention.

"O-o-o-o Popo! Popo! Popo!" rang

out the voice, with angry staccato insistence. "You Popo! Aw-w-w! you *Popo!*" Then, presently, "O-o-o-o! you Po-po-cat-e-petl!"

"Good heavens!" said Roden, bursting into laughter. "Is that really the poor little devil's name?"

"Mh—mh," said Virginia, with a nod of assent. "There was three of 'em born all to oncet. One's called Popocatepetl, an' one Iztaccihuatl, an' one Orizaba. We call 'em Popo, an' Whattle, an' Zabe."

"That triumvirate ought to rule something," said Roden. "Could a nigger ever be President, Miss Virginia? What a lark it would be to speak of President Popocatepetl! What's the other name?"

"Page," said Miss Herrick.

"Page!" echoed the young Englishman —"*Page?* why surely that name belongs to the 'F.F.V.'s,' doesn't it?"

"All the darkies took th' name o' th' fam'lies they b'longed to after th' war," she explained. "I had a cook here oncet called Faginia Herrick; she used to b'long to father 'fo' th' war."

"By gad!" was Roden's sole remark. "By *gad!*" said he again.

"*You* needn't say nothin'!" she exclaimed, breaking suddenly into her melodious laughter; "there's two little right *black* niggers at th' mill, an' one's called Prince Albert and th' other Queen Victoria, 'n' 'f you leave off th' 'Prince' or th' 'Queen' they won't answer you, neether."

She was evidently delighted with his expression of face at this, and released the two dogs in order to indulge more freely in her mirthful mood. She sat down on the stone steps, letting her arms hang simply at her sides, and putting down her head, laughed into the hollow lap of her gray kirtle, as though confiding her surplus merriment to its care.

It was at this moment that the overseer came into sight—a tall, gaunt man, with a beard that seemed flying away with his round head, after the fashion of a comet's tail; little steely blue eyes drawing close to the bridge of his nose as though it magnetized them; long, crooked teeth, not unlike the palings in one of his own fences for tint and irregularity; and a wide-open square smile, like the smile of a Greek comic mask. He wore a waistcoat of as many hues as Joseph's renowned garment, a blue cotton shirt, ginger-colored trousers tucked into heavy mud-crusted boots, and a straw hat, impossible to describe, tilted to the back of his head. In his arms he carried the little black-and-tan terrier which Roden remembered, and twisted its untrimmed ears while talking.

"Howdy? howdy?" he remarked, genially. "My darter Faginia's tole me 'bout you. Got all yo' clo'es lef' in Washin'ton? Hey? Got 'em this mornin'? You don' sesso? Well! My darter Faginia says as how you're goin' in fur horse-racin'? That so? You don' sesso? Well, what d'you think er my darter Faginia, anyhow? Darter, go 'n' bring me some water; I'm mortal thirsty." Then, as the girl disappeared, "Well, what d'you think er her?"

"She seems to me very — very charming," ventured Roden.

"Well, sir, you 'ain't got no more idea of th' sweethearts that girl's had — I mean would 'a' had 'f I'd 'lowed it. The las' one was Jim Murdoch, a hoop-pole man. But, sir"— here Mr. Herrick assumed a tone of the most pompous dignity — "but I will tole you, sir, as how my darter Faginia shall deceive *no* retentions, *respecially* from a hoop-pole man!"

"A hoop-pole man?" said Roden.

"That thar's hit, sir, an' I cert'n'y means what I says," replied the overseer, relapsing again into his former slipshod easiness of speech and manner. "Consequently were, the beauty of the question air my darter

Faginia won't get married twel she gets a mighty good offer."

"I should say you were perfectly right," assented Roden.

"Well, yes, sir; I should sesso. I s'pose you ain't married, air you?"

"No. Do I look very like a married man?" said Roden, who continued to be amused. He thought the overseer almost as interesting as Virginia.

"Well, no," assented old Herrick, manipulating his abundant beard with an air of deep thought. "But the beauty of the question air, you kyarn't al'uz tell. Them as looks the mostest married gen'-ly ain't. An' contrarywise, them as don't, air—"

"Married?" said Roden.

"Well, considerbul, mostly," said the overseer.

Here Virginia returned with a gourd of water, keeping the quick-falling drops from her father's not too immaculate attire while he drank by means of her skilfully hollowed hands.

"Yo' breakfas' 's ready," she said over her shoulder to Roden. He went in, and found it to be a slight variation on the last night's meal. There were some corn-meal cakes — batter cakes, Virginia called them — and miraculously cooked mutton-chops. A half-hour later the overseer appeared at the window to offer his services as guide over the farm.

When Roden returned from his investigations it was one of the great clock in the hall, and the sky like a vast blue banner overhead.

He went out on the "front porch," and called to Herrick as he crossed "the yard," with the little terrier at his heels. "Is there a good view from that hill just back of the house?" he asked.

"Mos' people goes fyar crazy over it," said Herrick. "Hit's a right rough climb to the top. Want tuh go up? Faginia kin show you. O-o-o-o-o Faginia! Faginia!"

Virginia appeared, clad from throat to heels in a vast brown apron, her half-bare arms covered with flour, and her thick braids skewered across the top of her head with a big wooden knitting-needle.

"Makin' bread?" said her father. "Well, yo' kin get yo' mammy to finish that. Mr. Roden here he wants to go trapeezing up to th' top o' Peter's Mountain. I tole him you could show him."

"All right," she said, briefly; "but I kyarn't walk: the Alderney heifer stepped on my foot this mornin'. I'll ride if you like:" this last to Roden.

"By all means," he said; "but if you do not mind, I had rather walk."

"Of co'se," she said, and disappeared again.

"The beauty of the question air," said her sire, looking proudly after her, "that gyrl kin ride like a Injun."

"She seems to do everything well," said Roden, with a pleased recollection of those mutton-chops which Aunt Tishy had confided to him "Miss Faginia done herself."

"She cert'n'y does," said Herrick, and after making some unique excuse disappeared also.

Miss Herrick appeared a few moments later, again clad in her boyish attire, and mounted upon a fidgety little roan mare. She had slung a wicker basket from the saddle, and Roden heard a merry clink as of glass kissing silver when the mare sidled about.

"That's a clever-looking little nag," said Roden. "Is she yours?"

"Nuck," said Virginia. "I reckon she's yours; she goes with the place."

"I didn't see her this morning," Roden said, somewhat puzzled.

"No; she'd gone to the shop to get a new shoe; that's why. I reckon you'll name her over."

"Why?" said Roden. It seemed to him he had never put that monosyllabic question so often before in the entire course of his life.

"'Cause it ain't very pretty," Virginia explained. "Father named her—it's Pokeberry."

"Oh, I don't know," said Roden, laughing. "I rather fancy it. It's uncommon, to say the least. I don't think I'll change it."

"Well, there's two others I *know* you'll change," she asserted. "They're two carriage-horses, an' they're named Peckerwood an' Hoppergrass."

"Capital!" said Roden, laughing again. "Change them?—not much! Shall we start now?"

It was a perfect day—perfect as only a day in Southern winter-tide can be. The air was radiant, wine-like, while with a still further suggestiveness little glittering insects spun around and around in the sunlight like the particles of gold-leaf in eau-de-vie de Dantzic. The roads, dried in some sort by the steady wind of the past night and morning, were mellowed to a dull orange in lieu of their former startling crimson. Infinite tones of faded browns and grays wrapped wold and hill-side. The sky, of an intense metallic pallor, was covered with gauze-like masses of wind-torn cirri. As they went on, a sycamore thrust its bone-white arms before a dark hollow in the mountain-side, reminding one of a skeleton guarding the mouth of a cavern, where during its life it had concealed some treasure. The harsh call of crows, beginning in the far east, passed in *crescendo* above their heads, and died away as the heavy birds flew westward.

Virginia, apparently unconscious of his presence, was watching Roden narrowly as he walked at her side. Owing to that peculiar faculty with which only women are endowed, she was enabled thus to observe him while seemingly absorbed in the sun-shot vista of the road before them. He had taken off his coat, as the increasing sunlight and the exertion of walking had overheated him, and his flannel shirt expressed damply the splendid modelling of his supple body. She noticed how the sun-burn stopped in a line about his throat, the fair flesh showing beneath with a girlish whiteness, as is often the case with very strong men.

"It's a heap whiter than mine," thought Virginia.

"I wish you'd sing," he said, suddenly. "Will you?"

"A nigger song?" said the girl, with a growing intuition in regard to his wishes. She then sang as follows:

"Bright sunny mornin'
Nigger feel good,
Axe on he shoulder
Goin' fur de wood.
Little piece er hoe-cake
'Thout any fat;

White folks quoil
  'Case he eat all o' dat.
    Hop 'long, hop 'long, hop 'long, Peter,
      Hop 'long, Peter's son!
    Hoppergrass sittin' on a sweet-e'ayter vine,
      Big tuckey-gorbler come up behine,
    Hop 'long, Peter's son.

"One bright mornin' John did go
Down in de medder fur ter mow;
Ez he mowed acrost de fiel'
Great big sarpint bit him on de heel.
He juck it up right in he hand,
And back he went tuh Maury Ann;
'Oh, Maury Ann, oh, don' you see,
One ole sarpint done bit me!'
    Hop 'long, hop 'long, hop 'long, Peter,
      Hop 'long, Peter's son."

Roden was delighted with her rich, reed-noted voice. She imitated the negroes' tones to perfection. The inflection and intonation were without fault.

"How well you do it!" he said. "It's really awfully pretty. Can't you give me another?"

She sang him one or two more, and ended by repeating in a singsong fashion a little rhyme which convulsed him:

> "Mars'r had a leetle dorg,
>   An' he was three parts houn';
> Ev'y time he strike a trail
>   He bounce up off de groun'."

"They make up all these things, of course?" he asked her.

"Oh yes," said Virginia: "they're awful fond of 'makin' hymes,' as they call it. Here's another:

> "Ef I had a needle an' thread,
>   Big ez I could sew,
> I'd stitch my 'Liza to my side,
>   An' off down de road I'd go."

He amused himself by trying to sing some of the various ditties after her, but, as they began to ascend the mountain, found that he needed all the breath at his command.

The dead leaves, sodden with the winter rains, closed in masses about the feet of Pokeberry, and of the young Englishman as he tramped untiringly at her muzzle. The shaft of a young pine rose slender and virginal from the lace-work of bare trees, its plumy crest breaking with lucent emerald the sea-blue reach of sky. A cardinal-bird flashed, with unconscious contrast, against the neutral tints of the woody distance, meshed as it were in the multitudinous glittering of sunlit twigs. From the leaf-stirred silence, far in the heart of the forest, came the urgent rat-a-plan of a woodpecker. Dead leaves occasionally, loosened by the fitful wind, fell, turning slowly in their descent, now between the startled ears of Pokeberry, themselves most leaf-like, now upon Virginia's skirt or hat, as she sat wordless, listlessly supporting the reins upon her knee.

They came presently to a narrow mountain stream, clear and brown, over the sunken leaves. The sunlight through the swaying tendrils of a wild grape-vine overhead sent dim but sharply defined shadows wavering back and forth over its bright surface, as though, being spiritualized, they breathed with a new life. A corn-crake, moving cautiously among the withered water-grasses, thrust forward its gay crest and peered inquisitively at them, whereupon the collie cleared the brook with an arching bound, and set forth in mad pursuit of this new quarry. The crake at once rose into the blue lift, with the harsh, derisive cry from which it takes its name.

After a while they came upon a log-cabin set in a little patch of cleared ground. From a small window close against the roof flaunted a mud-stained curtain of sacking. The red clay marks responded to a certain morbidness in Virginia, by suggesting the wiping of bloody hands upon the coarse stuff. There had been a murder some years before on this very mountain, and thoughts of a grewsome sort were easily called forth in her when remembering. A few black-and-white pigs of the genus "nigger" hurtled squealing down the hill-side, pursued by the indefatigable collie, while a little fawn-colored child, with whity-brown hair and purplish-white eyes, stood in the door and apparently bit its thumb at them.

"Do you bite your thumb at us, sir?" quoted Roden, cheerily, whereat the little darky fled, with a shrill "Yah!" of mingled delight and terror, into the bacon-perfumed room beyond.

They were now stopped by some draw-bars, which passed, they found themselves ascending a steep incline sown with large stones, as though Jove and his giants might have had a sharp encounter just in that spot. But having gained the top of the bluff, they came upon a view at which Roden stood and stared in silent admiration. It seemed to him that he had never before so entirely realized the ball-like character of the earth. It seemed now to be swinging like a magician's globe, imprisoned in another of larger size, which was hollowed from some marvellous, million-colored gem.

The air had changed suddenly from balmy warmth to a strange damp keenness, while the sky, which had cleared on their way up, was strewn from east to west with the same woolly clouds which had at first covered it. All above them was a lustrous monotone of gray, brightening towards the east into a pale daffodil, and farther towards the south into a lurid orange. From south to west a band of vivid violet-blue stretched solidly, cleft here and there with wedges of pale light slanting in regular order, like the bayonets of a vast army marching eastward.

"That," said Virginia, indicating the gorgeous phenomenon, "means rain."

"Oh, I think not," said Roden, carelessly.

"Very well," said Miss Herrick.

The wind blew ever stronger and stronger from the north, shifting suddenly to the north-east. Virginia felt a heavy splash of water upon her hand. She said nothing, but held it out to Roden in silence, and at the same moment the wind, scolding like an old hag who has been deprived by some adventurous urchin of her dinner, bore down upon them.

"Never mind," said Roden, "we are only about a quarter of a mile from the top."

"Won't you put on your coat now?" said Virginia, blinded by the blowing of her hair into her eyes.

He replied that he did not feel the need of it, and strode on a little ahead. The wind sent his shirt in fine ripples across his back. One could distinctly see the muscles at work beneath the flexible skin. Strength, above all things, was what this little barbarian admired, and she saw it now in a perfection which filled her with unconscious satisfaction.

"My! couldn't he double that braggin' Joe Scott up!" she told herself. "Whew!

I'd like to see somebody make him right mad. Couldn't he lick 'em!"

As they neared the summit the gale became more furious. Roden was obliged to lead the thoroughly frightened mare, and Virginia's long hair, becoming unbound, whipped with the sting of a lash across his face. She recaptured and held it firmly with one hand, while he, furtively observing it, thought it must be at least two yards in length. She assumed a new phase in his eyes, wrapped thus in her plenteous tresses. A certain boyish look, transmitted to her through the medium of the short locks about her brow, had vanished completely. She looked like some mountain Godiva hidden all as in a banner of cloth of gold. Roden wondered if such marvellous hair was a characteristic of Southern women.

They came at last to the one stunted apple-tree which crowned the noble crest of the mountain, with an effect as bathetic as the scalp-lock of an Indian brave. The wind screamed through the gnarled ground-kissing branches with the sound of a gale through cordage. Pokeberry squatted ignominiously in the fierce hurly, and put back her nervous ears, while Virginia swung from the saddle. Once on the ground, she found that to keep the perpendicular was a matter of some skill. She put one arm around a mass of the tangled branches and looked up at Roden with a laugh, which was seized and dashed down the steep declivity or ever it reached his ears. He in the mean time having tethered the mare securely, resumed his coat, and unbinding his covert-coat from the saddle, offered to help the girl on with it. She looked at him in evident surprise, but made no resistance. As she loosened the branches in order to put her arms into the sleeves, which were whirling wildly, with an air of reckless intoxication, a sharp gust blew her, coat and all, directly into Roden's arms.

He laughed, disentangling himself as

best he might from the wet bondage of her heavy locks, but she, reddening vividly through all her clear, sun-browned skin, gave her attention to the garment that he held. It seemed to her a strange thing that he should offer to lend it. She had been on rainy expeditions with many men, both English and Virginian, while none that she could remember had ever before offered to protect her in such wise from the inclemency of her native heavens.

She looked down a little consciously at the weather-stained tan-color of the little coat. She felt that it would be an insult to suggest to so mighty a pedestrian the idea of taking cold; at the same time she was afraid that such would be the memento he would bear away with him from the top of Peter's Mountain. As for herself, she was as accustomed to wind and rain as one of the big oxeye daisies in her own fields.

"There's some sandwiches an' a glass in that basket," she said, or rather shrieked,

ON THE TOP OF PETER'S MOUNTAIN.

to Roden. He went to get them, tacking through the stiff wind with much dexterity, and they partook of thin slices of Aunt Tishy's bread and Virginian ham with a heroic disregard of the downpour. All at once they were confronted by a small ebon figure, hatless and breathless.

"*Popo!*" said Miss Herrick; "what in the name o' sense are you doin' here?"

"Oh, Miss Faginia, Miss Faginia," howled the little black, "de lightnin' dun gone thoo Marse Johnson's house an' kill he an' he horg! An' I wuz so skeered 'bout you I jess took out an' run up de mounting to see ef you wuz all right."

"Well, I am," said his mistress. "You pore little thing, how wet you are! Come and get here under these branches."

The faithful Popocatepetl came and crouched on his heels at her side. He was drenched to the skin, and his dark hide showed in patches through his shirt of some thin white stuff, which elsewhere puffed out in irregular blisters, like the wet linen in a washer-woman's tub. From a strange freak of nature, not unusual in these Virginian mountains, his knotty wool was of a pale tan-color. It is a mistake to think that the little negro perpetually grins. Nothing absolutely could have been more full of woe and resignation than the expression of the young Popo as he watched with Pokeberry the ceaseless flood that swept over hill and valley.

Although comparatively sheltered, there still escaped through the tangled apple-boughs moisture sufficient to prove extremely unpleasant. The large drops fell heavy and monotonous, some into the furry hollows of the mare's flexile ears, causing her to toss her head with a swift impatience of movement that set the little metal buckles on her head-gear tinkling faintly, some upon Roden's breast and hands, some upon the uncovered head and cheeks of the girl at his side. She tossed her head once or twice with a close reproduction of Pokeberry's impulsive gestures.

The surrounding mountains were by this time entirely blotted from sight by the lead-colored sheets of wind-urged rain. The branches of the trees on the slopes below them seemed living creatures, who, frantic with alarm, tugged and twisted to free themselves from their native boles, and to flee before the ruffian wind that assaulted them. Blown leaves, like troops of frightened birds, were driven past in gusts. Not a sound was to be heard save the ceaseless hiss of the rain on the hard ground, the creaking of the tortured trees, and the fluctuating roar of the wind above all else. Pokeberry, cowed and shivering, gazed wistfully down at the swimming field below.

The darkness had increased palpably within the last five minutes, and the wind, raging downward through the stems of the tall pines on the eastern slope of the mountain, made a sound like to the angry breathing of some giant through his locked teeth.

"That is almost wolfish," said Roden.

"There *was* wolves in these mountains when my father was a little boy," she responded.

Darker clouds seemed to be ever rolling up from the east, veined with glittering threads of lightning, which pierced the irregular masses on all sides like the fronds of an immense leaf. The trees on the slopes, still wind-swept, seemed anon pale with terror or dark with dread as their light and dark leaves were alternately tossed upward. Over against the west was a dull citrine glare, like the smoke that overhangs a battle-field on a sunlit day, reflected here and there in the slimy soil and rain-roughened waters of a stream some way beneath them.

Suddenly Virginia turned and swung out of Roden's coat with one of her swift movements. "Please put it on," she said to him.

"Why, no," he said; "I don't want it. I'm

perfectly comfortable. I don't know why I brought it—unless from a happy inspiration in regard to you," he added, pleasantly. She turned from him, and stooping, wrapped the shivering Popo in it.

"They feel the cole so!" she said to Roden, standing erect again. "An' I never wrop up." Roden did not know whether to laugh or to swear.

When the rain had abated somewhat, and they returned to Caryston, he told himself, as he soothed his inner man with some excellent Scotch whiskey, that he "really rather liked it in the girl; but—d——n the little nigger!—that was my pet coat!"

III.

Roden was the younger son of an Englishman of title. He was also what is sometimes graphically described as being *sans le sou*. It was his intention to try stud-farming in Virginia. No better horseman than Roden ever put boot in stirrup. He had, as an old pad-groom once remarked, "a genus for osses." It was a mania, a fad of the most pronounced type, with him. No woman's eye had ever possessed for him half the charm that did the full orbs of his favorite mare, Bonnibel, as she gazed lustrously upon him over her well-filled manger. No sheen of woman's hair had ever vied, in his opinion, with the satin flanks of Bonnibel. What was it to love a woman? Was it half the zest, the delight, of feeling a good horse between one's knees, what time the welcome cry of "Gone away!" makes glad delirium in one's veins, while the music of the spotted darlings thrills air and soul? Roden would bluntly and unpoetically have informed you that you were a "duffer" had you attempted to argue the point. He had never cared much for women, either collectively or as individuals. They had perhaps played too small a part in his life. "Egad, sir!" his father had cried to him one day in a fit of anger, "you'll grow up with a pair of legs like pot-hooks!"

Mr. Herrick informed him, on the second day after his arrival, that "the beauty of the question were, he cert'n'y did have a mighty good foothold on a hawse."

It was on that day also that most of the horses arrived from New York—Bonnibel among them. She was as beautiful a daughter as Norseman ever sired. Deep of girth, clean of limb, broad of loin, with splendid oblique shoulders, bossed with sinew and muscle which quivered with restrained power beneath the silky, supple hide; a small compact head with ample front, over which the sensitive leaf-like ears kept restless guard; great limpid eyes, a crest like a rainbow, and quarters to have lifted Leander clean over the Hellespont. In color she was a rich brown, touched with tan on muzzle and flanks, while the slight floss of mane and tail had also flecks of gold towards the ends, like those in the locks of some dark-haired women. Like her great-granddam, Fleur-de-Lis, she stood full sixteen hands, but was neither leggy nor light of bone.

"May I give her an apple?" said Virginia, as she turned her slow, dark look from Bonnibel to her master. That sagacious damosel was already reaching after the coveted golden ball in the girl's hand, with cajoling little movements of her soft nose. Having obtained permission, Miss Herrick threw one arm over the mare's graceful crest and presented her with the apple—one of those renowned Albemarle pippins on which no duty is demanded by England's gracious queen.

Bonnibel ate it with evident participation in her sovereign's good taste, rubbing her handsome head against the girl's arm with an almost cat-like softness of caress.

"I don' s'pose any one ever rides her but you?" said Virginia, with a suggestion of wistfulness in her low voice.

"Well, no," said Roden; "only the lad who gives her her gallops. She is as kind as a kitten, but rather hot-headed and excitable. Why do you ask? Would you like to ride her?"

"Yes, of co'se I would," said the girl, calmly; "but you needn't bother; I know how Englishmen are 'bout their horses. Some time, if the boy as rides her gets sick, if you'll let me I'll show you whether I kin ride or no."

"Your father says you ride like an Indian," said Roden.

She moved her shoulders beneath her loose gray jacket with something very like a shrug. "I don't bleeve father ever saw a Injun in his life," she remarked. "You wait; I'll show you."

"I don't doubt you have a good seat," said Roden, pleasantly; he took particular pains to speak pleasantly always to Herrick and his daughter. "But the chief thing with a horse like Bonnibel is the hands. How are you about that?"

"How do you mean?" she said, puzzled.

"Why, have you nice light hands? Are you gentle in handling your mount?"

"Oh," she said, with the comprehensive indrawing of the breath which he was beginning to recognize as one of her chief characteristics. "You mean am I kind about yerkin' 'em. Well, I'll tell you: I never pulled any rougher on a horse's mouth in my life than I'd like anybody to pull on mine."

"I wish some of my friends would take

that for their motto," said Roden. "I'm thinking I'll let you ride Bonnibel some time, if *she* will." He ended with a smile.

It was not more than a week afterwards that he had occasion to require Virginia's services. One of the other horses, a rank, irritable brute, called Usurper, had jammed Roden's shoulder quite severely against the side of the box, and Bonnibel's own especial groom had been sent back to New York to bring on two new-comers but just arrived from England.

"I don't think she'll stand a riding-skirt," he said, rather doubtfully, as the beautiful beast was led out, reaching after the reins with her supple neck.

"I ain't goin' to ride her with one," said Virginia.

He then saw that Bonnibel was saddled with a man's saddle, and the next moment the girl was astride of the mare, the reins gathered skilfully into her long brown fingers, head erect, and hands well down—

lithe, beautiful with the beauty of some sunburnt, mountain-bred boy.

As Bonnibel felt the strange touch upon her mouth she wheeled, rearing a little, and the girl's soft hat was shaken from her head. Roden wondered if he had ever seen anything prettier than the sunlight on the young Virginian's sun-like curls, and the glossy hide of Bonnibel.

The mare was going quieter now, mincing along and picking up her feet after a fashion much in vogue among equine coquettes. She was beginning to like the feel of the light, firm hands, and to be sensible of the masterly pressure of the strong young knees upon her mighty shoulders.

"By Jove! what a graceful seat the little witch has got!" Roden said to himself with sufficient admiration. "And hands as steady as an old stager!—Gad!" This exclamation, breaking forth at first from an impulse of terror, ended in the relieved announcement, "That was fine; as I live it was!"

Bonnibel had bolted, going straight for a snake-fence at the bottom of the hill on which the stables were builded. To stop her was, he knew, impossible; to turn her aside on the slippery turf, more unreliable than usual with the spring rains, would have been culpably perilous. The fence just here was fortunately not very high, but Bonnibel had one serious fault. When excited, she had a way of going at her fences head down, after a fashion calculated to break her own neck, and certainly that of the person who rode her. He saw the girl sit well down in the saddle, run the bit through the mare's mouth, and bring her head up, showing her the leap in front with a skill he could not himself have rivalled; and Roden was no tyro. Bonnibel cleared the rails in gallant form, and Virginia then took her for a canter around the field beyond.

She came up to Roden, ten minutes later, with flushed cheeks and her great eyes brilliant.

"If she had a-hurt herself then," she said, flinging herself tempestuously to the ground, "I'd 'a' got one o' th' grooms to kill me." She turned and showered the mare's sleek crest with kisses, then tossed the reins to Roden, and ran swiftly out of sight towards the house. He thought her the strangest creature he had ever seen.

In the mean time the days wore on. Roden was more than pleased with his Virginian venture. He had three excellent stables building, his gees were all in first-rate condition, and his prospect for the provincial races more than fair.

Virginia now rode Bonnibel every day. There sprung up between the two, mare and woman, one of those mutual attachments as rare in reality as they are common in fiction. Virginia could catch the nervous beast when it meant danger to others to come within reach of her iron-shod heels. Virginia seemed to murmur a strange language into her slender ears, as certain in its effects as the whisper of the Roumanians to their horses. For Virginia would Bonnibel become as a spring lamb for meekness, or one of her own mountain-streams for impetuosity. It afforded Roden a strange pleasure to watch the relations which existed between this beautiful savage maiden and his beautiful savage mare.

On the other hand, he found the girl more than useful to him. She knew all the owners of good horse-flesh in the surrounding counties. She explored strange woods with him, while it came to be an understood thing that every day she should go with him on his long tramps. She marched sturdily at his side through brake and brier. She had no skirts to tear, no under-draperies of lace to draggle. She was always good-tempered and never tired.

It was one day about the middle of March that they stood together on a wind-blown hill-side. A dark-blue sky gleamed overhead, set thickly with clouds of a vivid, opaque white, like the figures on antique Etruscan ware. The chain of distant hills clasped the tawny winter earth, as a violet ribbon might clasp the dusky body of an Eastern slave. So like was the pale horizon to a sunlit sea that the white gleam of a wood-dove's wing across it suggested instantly to them both the idea of a sail.

There was a sound, now far, now near, vague, intermittent, made by the rushing of the wind through the dry grass in the fields. The forlorn discord of the voices of spring lambs reached their ears, together with the reassuring monotone of the ewes. A sudden commotion among the flock caused Virginia to run suddenly forward, shading her eyes with her hand.

"It's that narsty Erroll dorg again!" she

said, wrathfully. "He'll jess run those sheep to death."

"What dog?" said Roden, coming up beside her. "By Jove! it's a German sleuth-hound," he added. "I'm afraid he'll play the deuce with your father's sheep, Miss Virginia."

"He will so, ef he ain't stopped," she said, gloomily. "I didn't know the Errolls had come back to Windemere. Plague gone him! Look there, now!"

Just here came the shrill sound of a dog-whistle, then a clear voice calling, "Laurin! Laurin! Laurin, I say!"

They saw a girl on a chestnut horse, galloping towards the terrified, bleating sheep. She gained upon the great hound, came up with him, swung from her saddle, and caught him by the collar. After a moment or two she began to walk towards them through the weeds and brambles which overgrew the hill-side. As she came nearer they could see that she held a lamb beneath one arm. A tall, slight girl in a dark habit, with dark curls escaping about her forehead from her very correct pot hat. The hound followed meekly. "I am so very, very sorry," she called out, while yet some distance off. "I am afraid my dog has hurt this poor little thing." As she came closer Roden saw that there was blood on the lamb, and on the dog's dripping jaws.

"Please look at it," the girl said, wofully. "I'm afraid nothing will ever break him. He will have to be sent away. They are your father's sheep, aren't they, Miss Herrick—you are Miss Herrick?"

Virginia lifted her full look to the stranger's face. "Yes, that's my name," she answered. "Why don't you muzzle him, or keep him chained? He'll get shot some day."

The girl looked sadly down at her huge pet. "I'm afraid he will," she said, gently. "I wish he wouldn't do it. I can't feel the same to him. Ah, you beast!"—this last to the recreant Laurin, in a tone of wrath. In the mean time Roden had finished his examination of the lamb.

"I don't think it's serious," he said, kindly; "but it will have to be looked after a bit. Miss Herrick here will doctor it successfully, I've no doubt."

"Oh, couldn't I have it?" said the girl, eagerly. "I'm such a good hand at curing things. Do let me have it, Miss Herrick."

"Take it if you want it," said Virginia.

"But cannot you have it sent?" said Roden, as the girl held out her hand for the lamb. "I am afraid you will get blood all over your habit, Miss—" He had not meant to fish for her name, and stopped abruptly.

She looked at him with a soft smiling of lips and eyes. "My name is Erroll— Mary Erroll," she said. "And thank you, I would rather take it. Laurin will follow me now. *Ah*, you beast!"

"You will have to put it down until you mount," said Roden, laughing a little in spite of himself, as the old lines about Mary and her little lamb crossed his mind.

"Oh no, I wouldn't put it down," she said, hastily. "Miss Herrick will hold it for me, won't you?—and if you would be so kind as to mount me, Mr. Roden."

"You know my name?" said Roden, as he took the slight foot, arched like Bonnibel's crest, into his hand.

"Why, who in the neighborhood does not?" she said, settling herself in the saddle. "Not to know you would be to argue one's self very much unknown in this neighborhood. Now give me the lamb. Thank you so much. Come, Laurin. Good-by, Miss Herrick." She placed the lamb carefully against her side, whistled to the hound, and started off at a round trot. Her figure, in its trim Quorn-cloth habit, came into bold relief against the vivid sky. He watched admiringly the long supple waist as it swayed to the motion of the horse, the bold graceful sweep of the shoulders, and high carriage of the small head. He had read so much concerning the gathers and gilt braid of the Virginian horsewoman that it struck him as something entirely strange, the fact that Miss Mary Erroll should wear a neat, well-cut habit, and a chimney-pot hat. He also recalled that her saddle was all that it should be, and that instead of the gold-and-ivory-handled cutting whip which he had been led to expect, she carried a light but sturdy crop.

"By Jove! how she rides!" he said to himself.

"Don't I ride as well?" came the soft monotone of Virginia at his ear.

He answered her, still with his eyes on the vanishing figure of the girl in the Quorn-cloth habit. "You ride like an Arab," he said. "She rides like—like—like an Englishwoman."

"You don't think I ride as well," said

Virginia, in an indescribable voice, turning away. She was filled with an unreasoning, unchristian, wholly uncivilized desire to mount Bonnibel, overtake, and spatter Miss Mary Erroll with as much mud as possible. Suddenly she turned and came back to Roden. "I—I—I s'pose you think a gyrl oughtn' to ride straddle?" she said, with an unusual hint of timidity in her rich tones.

"Oh, I don't know that there's any harm in it," he said, carelessly. Again she stood away from him. A feeling of utterly unreasonable anger and rebellion was swelling in her heart and straining her throat. Was it against Miss Mary Erroll or against Roden? She could not herself have told. One fact was entirely apparent to her: he did not deem what she did or did not do things worthy his consideration.

"I bet she couldn't ride Bonnibel!" she said, passionately, between her locked teeth, as she went blindly on through the furze and briers. "I bet she couldn't ride Bonnibel—straddle or no straddle!"

It was not until three days later that she found out from her father the fact of Roden's having been to call (nominally) upon the lamb of Miss Mary Erroll.

"The beauty of the question air," ended that modern Solomon, as he filled his white clay pipe — "The beauty of the question air, that thar gyrl cert'n'y is goin' to lead that young fellar a darnce. They say she's got it down ter a fine p'int."

"What?" said Virginia, curtly.

"Why, coquettin'—hyah! hyah! *That's* the darnce she'll lead *him*. 'N' they sez, moresomever, as how th' English fellars takes to her like the partridges ter th' woods—plague 'em!—'count o' her w'arin' boots like a man, an' skirts at harf-marst when she goes out on hawseback. Lawd! I cert'n'y do 'spise ter see a woman hitched onter th' side uv er hawse like a peckerwood a-stickin' ter rer tree-trunk!"

Virginia came and leaned on the back of his chair, picking some bits of straw from his many-hued waistcoat. "You don't think it's any harm for a girl to ride straddle, do you, father?" she said, slowly.

"Harm!" said old Herrick, twisting about in his chair to look up at her—"*harm!*" He set his pipe firmly between his teeth, and pushed out his underlip with an expression of entire scorn. "Is there any harm in a hoppergrass hoppin'?" he questioned. "G'long! don' talk none o' yo' nonsense ter me!"

This, however, did not entirely satisfy her on the question in point.

Roden was not a little astonished to meet her, as she returned from giving Bonnibel her morning gallop, in a very fair imitation of Miss Mary Erroll's habit, and an old pot hat that had evidently belonged to some one of the previous Englishmen.

"Why, what a swell you are!" he said, pleasantly, joining her. "But how does Bonnibel like the change?"

"It don't make any diff'r'nce how she likes it," said Miss Herrick, curtly, adding hastily, with a swift change of manner, "She r'ared once or twice at first, but that's all." Then she stopped suddenly, and stepped around in front of him. "How—how does it look—really?" she said, with a shamefaced and comprehensive downward glance at her skirt.

"It looks awfully well," Roden assured her—"awfully well. How tall and strong you are, Miss Virginia!"

"I've got a right good mustle," she said, showing her handsome teeth in one of her rare and vivid smiles. "Mornin': I've got a heap to do."

Roden watched her as she stalked away with her splendid swinging stride, thinking vaguely of her beauty and its absolute waste in her position. "She'll marry some 'po' white' who talks as much like a nigger as her own father," he thought, half regretfully; "have a lot of children, and end by smoking a pipe—ugh!" He then went to call, for the third time that week, upon Mary Erroll. The visit ended by their going for a ride, and just as they neared the gates of Caryston a smart shower came pelting down the eastern slope of Peter's Mountain.

"Do come in and wait until this is over," he said, urgently, bending from his horse to open the long gray gate, which was now proudly supported on strong hinges. "Miss Herrick will chaperon us."

"Why, of course I'll come," she said, amazed, in her Southern freedom, that he should pause to question the propriety of her so doing. At one o'clock in the day, and with her little darky henchman mounting guard, what possible objection could any one find? She ran up the stone steps with a pretty clattering of her boots, and Roden threw wide the doors of the great hall. She was delighted with everything; got on a chair to examine the great moose-head; struck some chords on an old harp that she discovered in a dark corner; made friends with the collie and one of the Persian cats, who came purring up from the recess of a distant window; looked over his collection of curious weapons; and on finding that he had spent some years of his life in Mexico, questioned him about his experiences there with a pretty assumption of almost motherly interest.

"Can't you say some—some Mexican?" she said. "I should so like to hear it."

"I love you, most beautiful of maidens," said Roden, lazily, in the Mexican patois.

"What does that mean? It sounds enchanting."

"It means enchantment."

She leaned suddenly forward and looked at him with her bright, soft, childishly chaste eyes. "Mr. Roden," she said, sweetly, "if I were not very sure you were only laughing, I should accuse you of trying to ensnare my simple country soul with a spurious sentimentality."

Roden roused himself from his lounging position in one of the big hall chairs with a jerk. An expression half of amusement, half of guilt, crossed his handsome sunburnt face. "You are very unjust," he said. "I am certainly not laughing, and I couldn't be sentimental if I tried."

"Oh! oh!" she said, with her pretty Southern accent. "How very, how rudely unflattering!"

"I meant I would not have to try to be so — with you," said Roden, dexterously mendacious.

"How very, how rudely untruthful!"

They were here told by Popocatepetl that "lunch dun rade-y."

Roden's meals were generally presided over by Virginia, and she came forward to meet him now with a little silver dish of apples in one hand, evidently utterly ignorant of the presence of Mary Erroll. She stopped short, half-way across the room. A shadow as definite and sombre as the shadow from a brilliant cloud upon a laughing grass-field in May settled over her face.

"I'll have to fix another place," she said, curtly, and turned her back upon them in order to do so.

Miss Erroll expressed herself charmed with her luncheon. She ate bread and honey with all the gusto of the queen of nursery lore, taking off her riding-gloves and showing long, flower-like hands, that were reflected as whitely in the polished mahogany of the round table as the pale primroses which adorned its centre.

Virginia moved about noiselessly. All at once she stopped beside Roden, and put one hand heavily on the back of his chair. He looked up in some surprise. Her eyes were flashing under her bent brows, like the "brush fires" of her native State under a night horizon.

"I'll wait on *you*," she said, in a smothered voice—"I say I'll wait on *you, but I won't wait on her.*" She dashed down his napkin, which she had lifted from the floor, and strode with her swift, noiseless movements to the door.

"Virginia!" said Roden, aghast—"Virginia!"

"I don't care!" cried the girl, passionately, swinging open the heavy door—"I don't care! I ain't anybody's nigger!"

She rushed out tempestuously, dragging from one or two rings the heavy portière, which with a native incongruity hung before the door itself.

"How vulgarity will crop out!" said Roden, rising to shut the door. "That poor little girl has behaved so well until to-day!"

That evening, as he sat writing in a little room opening into the dining-room, Virginia entered, and came and stood beside him. He did not look up. She had annoyed him a good deal, and he was not prepared to yield the forgiveness for which he felt she had come to plead. She stood there some moments quite silent, then reached over his shoulder and dropped something on the table before him.

"You said th' other day you wanted one for the silver. There 'tis," she said. She turned before he could speak, and left the room.

Lifting the crimson mass from the table, he saw that it was an old-fashioned purse of netted silk, secured by little steel rings. He recalled a speech which he had made a day or two ago concerning the inconvenience of modern purses as regarded silver currency. He started up and opened the door, calling the girl by name two or three times. No one answered, and he went down the hall and into Herrick's room.

The overseer was there, whittling something by the light of a smoking kerosene lamp. Aunt Tishy was there, grumbling to herself about "folks cuttin' trash all over de flo' fur her ter break her pore ole back over." The raccoon was very much there, as he seemed to be having a fit just as Roden entered. But there was no Virginia. Her spinning-wheel stood idle in its corner; her heavy boots were drying in front of the wood fire; there was a book, face down, upon the deal table—a book which she must have been reading, as no one else at Caryston besides Roden ever glanced between the covers of one.

He lifted it, expecting to find some Dora-Thornesque romance of high life. It was a condensed copy of "Youatt on the Horse," and beneath it was a racing calendar for '79. Alas! alas! even this discovery told nothing else to this otherwise discerning young man. He smiled as he put down the volumes, thinking that the little Virginian was bent on making him acknowledge her a superior horsewoman in all respects.

He then inquired of Herrick as to the whereabouts of Virginia. Neither the girl's father nor Aunt Tishy could tell him.

"If you'll lend me a pencil I'll just leave a note for her," he said, feeling instinctively that she would not care to have a message in regard to her little gift left with her father or the old negress.

He scribbled a few words on one of the fly-leaves of the racing calendar, tore it out, folded it securely, and handed it to Herrick.

"Please give that to your daughter when she comes back," he said. "Good-night," and left the room.

Old Herrick waited until he heard the distant clang of the dining-room door; then he settled his spectacles very carefully upon his large nose, pushed out his under-lip, and unfolding the little note, thrust it almost into the flame of the lamp while reading it.

"'Dear Miss Faginia' (Humph!),— 'Many thanks fur yo' beeyeutiful purse. I will alluz keep hit. Very truly yours,

"'J. Roden.'"

"Humph!" ejaculated Herrick again— "humph!"

He set one long, knotty hand back down against his side, and turned the bit of paper about scornfully between the thumb and forefinger of his other hand, regarding it the while over his spectacles. "Humph!" he said for the fourth time.

IV.

It was one o'clock on that same night. Virginia Herrick leaned with round bare arms on the table, above which hung a little oblong, old-fashioned mirror in a warped mahogany frame. The one candle on a little bracket at her right hand, brought out the clear tones in her face and throat and arms, and dived vividly into her masses of loosened hair; beyond her was a background of vague shadows; she looked from the tarnished mirror like a painting from its frame. Her eyes were sombre and heavy under their dark lids. The light falling down upon her sent long delicate shadows trembling upon her cheeks—shadows such as are made by the bending of summer grasses across a woman's white gown, and which in Virginia's case were cast by her thick, curled lashes.

She had taken off the waist of her homespun dress, and the folds of her much-gathered chemise assumed a silvery tone in the concentrated light. The contrast between the dead white of the stuff and the living white of her neck and arms was as perfect as when Southern peach-trees, blossoming before their time, are seen next day against vast fields of snow.

One of the Persian cats leaped with soft agility upon the table, and passed purring between the girl and her fair image in the dingy glass; she swept him from her way with one sure motion of her strong bare arm, and returned to her intent scrutiny of her own face.

The time passed on. A rat began an intermittent nibbling in the old wainscoting of the room; sharp, sudden noises were heard overhead; the fire died out in tinkling silence; a heavy shroud of semi-transparent tallow wrapped the one candle. Two o'clock had sounded through the hollow depths of the old house some time ago. Suddenly she spoke. "I wisht I knew ef I war pretty," she said. Then, with passionate reiterance, "I *wisht* I knew ef I war pretty."

The cat, hearing her voice, leaped again beside her, as if to answer; again she swept him to the floor. The soft, cushioned thud of his feet against the bare boards sounded quite distinctly upon the silence, so alert to catch every noise. "Oh, I wisht—I *wisht* I knew ef I war pretty," she said once more.

Poor little savage, you are pretty indeed —with a prettiness which civilization would give many of its privileges to possess. So, I doubt not, were fashioned the wood-nymphs of old, with strength and with health and with grace beyond all power of reproduction—even so have they gazed deep into their woodland lakes; and the lakes, did they not answer? Who but Beauty was ever mother of such curves and tints?

This time she put another question. "I wisht I knew ef—it—pleased—*him.*"

She had yielded up her secret to the old mirror, and to Hafiz—what better confidants? The one had no tongue; the other a tongue used only for lapping unlimited supplies of Alderney cream.

With a sudden movement she leaned forward and blew out the sputtering candle. She did not wish even her own eyes in the mirror to pry upon her.

Three days later Roden and Usurper figured in a hurdle race of some note in the neighborhood.

This Usurper was by King Tom, out of Uarda, and as rank a brute as ever went headlong at his hurdle, often taking off nearly a length too soon. Virginia, who had seen him day after day at his work, ventured timidly to suggest to Roden that one of the lads should ride the horse. He laughed, and told her he had thought her above that very ordinary failing of women

—nervousness. She said nothing more, turning short on her heel with the customary dissenting movement of her fine shoulders.

These races were to be quite a swell affair, and there were a good many carriages outside of the course. Miss Erroll and her mother, sunk deep in an old-fashioned landau, talked to Roden as he leaned on the side of the carriage, very brown and gallant in his racing-togs.

Virginia was seated on Pokeberry, not three yards off. She watched curiously each movement of Miss Erroll, dwelling with strained, wondering eyes upon her pretty wrinkled gloves; her close-fitting corsage of white serge; her little dark-red velvet toque; her parasol, a vivid arrangement of cream-color and red, which made a charming plaque-like background for her fair face; she also noticed the posy of blue and white flowers which was pinned on the left side against the white bodice of Miss Erroll. Roden's colors were blue and white. Virginia herself had a little knot of white and blue hyacinths on her riding-habit; she jerked them out with a savage movement, tossed them on the ground, and carefully guided the hoofs of Pokeberry upon them.

All unconscious was she that in her eyes, blue now with anger, and her cheeks so white with pain, she wore his colors whether she would or not.

There were two races before the one in which he rode. Then he went off to be weighed, and Virginia dismounted from Pokeberry, and gave a little nigger a cent or two to hold the mare.

She went and leaned against the railing, waiting for the start. All went well enough until the finish. Roden came sweeping down the homestretch in an easy canter, Usurper well in hand and going game as a pebble, and one more hurdle to jump.

Virginia held her breath; she had a horrible certainty that Usurper would refuse that last hurdle, or do something equally idiotic. Roden sent him at it in fine form. There was a second of expectancy, a smart crash, and then Usurper, scrambling heavily to his feet, tore off down the course, leaving a mass of blue and white half under the débris of the hurdle. The brute had not risen an inch, and had flung Roden headfirst into the hurdle, himself turning a complete somersault.

On came the other horses, ten of them, in full gallop. Mary Erroll stood on her feet, with a little broken cry. Some men, until now paralyzed with astonishment and horror, started forward; but swifter than all, unhesitating, strong of arm as of nerve, Herrick's daughter, diving beneath the rail, rushed out into the middle of the track, and seizing the senseless man beneath his arms dragged him by main force out of the way of the coming horses. The hoof of one of them, however, struck her on her left shoulder, taking a good bit of flesh and cloth clean away as though with a knife.

There was a good deal of blood about Roden's head—some at first thought that he was seriously injured. They carried him into a tent and sent for a surgeon. In an hour he was all right, however, and wrote a few words upon some little ivory tablets, sent him by Miss Erroll for that purpose, to assure her of his entire recovery. Mary then sent to ask if Miss Herrick would not be so very kind as to come and speak to her. The girl came, sullenly enough, touching from time to time the bandages about her left shoulder, as though restless under even so slight a restraint.

"I want to thank you so very, very much," said Mary, in her sweetest voice. She leaned far out of the landau and held out her hand to Virginia.

"What a' *you* thankin' me fur?" demanded the girl, fiercely, stepping backward from the extended hand. "*You* ain't got nothin' to thank me fur—have you?" she ended, with a sudden change from aggressiveness to appeal infinitely pathetic.

A swift red had dyed Mary's face at the first reception of her kindly meant advances. It faded out now, leaving her very pale.

"Every one who is a friend of Mr. Roden ought to thank you, if they do not," she said, with great dignity. "I am sorry I spoke, since it has been so disagreeable to you. Good-morning."

Virginia was dismissed—she felt it. The knowledge went scorching through her veins as kirsch through the veins of one not accustomed to its fire. She hated the girl with a mad, barbaric impulse, which was as much beyond her control as its tides are beyond the control of the ocean; she felt an animosity to Miss Erroll's very hat, to her pretty parasol with its bunch of red velvet ribbons on the bamboo handle. She would have liked to seize and tear them to pieces, as a humming-bird tears the flower which has refused its honey. A red mist rose to her eyes. The Erroll carriage and its occupants seemed to be melting away and away in a golden haze. She stepped backward, keeping her eyes on it, as a fascinated bird looks ever on the serpent that has charmed it.

"I hate her—I hate her—I hate her," she said, back of her teeth, not fiercely, as she had at first spoken, but with a dull assertiveness.

She refused several offers from kindly neighbors who would have driven her home. She could ride quite well, she said, without using her left arm.

The evening was lowering and purple towards the north-east, full of vague shadows and noises of homeward creatures. The west was aglare as with floating golden ribbons from some mighty, unseen Maypole behind the luridly dark mountains.

The slanting light touched the crests of the clods in a newly ploughed field to her left with a vivid effect, remindful of the light-capped wavelets on an evening bay. Farther on it was long, glistening stalks of fodder which caught the level gleaming from the west, as might the rifles of a regiment that has been ordered to fire lying down. The fresh green hollows of the hills were full of a palpable golden ether, like cups of emerald brimmed with the lucent amber drink of other days.

A leather-winged bat brushed against her cheek, flying heavily into some broomstraw just beyond. She saw nothing, felt nothing, heard nothing beyond the dark hours ahead of her, the heavy aching of her heart, and its loud monotonous beating, to which she unconsciously set words as one does to the iterant chatter of a clock.

"Yes, he loves her—yes, he loves her," so it seemed to say, over and over, again and again. Almost she could have torn it from her breast and flung it from her, had not it been sacred to her for the love of him with which it was filled. Think of it; try to imagine it. A woman fully developed, heart and body full of the South from bright head to nimble feet, as the South is full of beauty; free as the birds that cleaved her native air with strong, untiring wings; unlearned in all emotion whether of love or of hate; not weary in sense or perception; untutored, unknowing, uncivilized—and loving for the first time in all her one-and-twenty years of living!

There was no analysis here, no picking to pieces of little emotions, no skewering of butterfly passions to sheets of paper from the book of former knowledge. No comparison between then and now — between now and what might possibly have been had the bits of glass in the kaleidoscope of existence assumed a certain difference of juxtaposition. She loved him. Why she loved him, how she loved him, she could no more have told you than she could have told the names of the different elements which composed the tears with which her hot eyes brimmed.

It was seven o'clock of that same evening. Roden, restless and feverish, flung from side to side on an old leathern sofa in the library. There were no candles, but a great fire of chestnut-wood sought and found all such points as were capable of illumination in the sombre old room—the brass claw feet of the tables and chairs, the great brass hinges of the rosewood bookcase, the glass knobs on an old writing-desk in one corner, Roden's eyes and hair as he lay listlessly resigned for a moment or two staring into the noisy labyrinths of the flames.

It was half an hour later. The leaping flames had settled as in sleep upon a bed of red-gold coals; a little ever-ascending spiral of gray-white smoke escaped from a cleft in the end of one of the half-burned logs. The old chimney-place was like a vivid picture set in the dark wall. Its yawning black throat, heavily clogged with soot, was tinged faintly for some way up by the glow from the lurid mass on the hearth. The great iron fire-dogs, at least four feet in height, were connected from shaft to shaft by a chain in grotesque suggestion of the Siamese twins. The much-burnt bricks had assumed opaline tones, in rosy grays and greenish-yellows, beneath the intense heat and light. On the hearth-rug the collie lay stretched, his ruffled legs every now and then executing an unavailing canter, as in his dreams perchance he chased a soaring buzzard.

They were all three asleep—the fire, the collie, Roden. A soft crooning wind, conducive to slumber, sighed at the doors and windows, vibrating every once in a while with sonorous minor cadences.

Suddenly the incessant monotone was snapped, as it were, to silence. The door leading into the library had been opened; some one entered cautiously, stood still;

then the door was again closed noiselessly.

The person who had entered crept forward a pace or two. It was Virginia. She had not yet taken off her riding-habit, and the bandages were yet about her shoulder. Some dark stains here and there told where the blood had soaked through. As she came forward, nearer to the rich lambency of the fire, her white face borrowed some of its roseate flush, but the lines of pain, mental and physical, were traced as with a fine chisel about the sombre mouth and eyes. Stealing past the foot of the sofa on which Roden lay, she stood a moment looking at him. Her crossed wrists pressed each other hard against her bosom, her long fingers drawing the stuff of her habit in wrinkles with the tenseness of their grasp upon it. Her breast rose and fell, impatient, eager, behind the close prison of her arms, as some woodland thing so held might seek to be free. All at once she sank down to her knees upon the hearth-rug, lifting both hands to her bent face, and rocking herself to and fro with wild, swaying movements of her supple body. The collie raised his head with a drowsy curiosity, and let it fall heavily again upon the floor. The varying monody of the wind had begun again through the chinks in the closed door.

At last she lifted her head, letting her clasped hands fall loosely into her lap. A sudden flame showed her with an added vividness the face of Roden as he lay in tired unconsciousness upon the old lounge. She moved nearer to him, still on her knees; then again lifting her hands to her bosom, leaned forward and gazed upon him as though one should drink with the eyes. Her great braids, ruffled and half unplaited, followed the lithe curves of her back with glittering undulations, as of two mated golden serpents. So passed some moments.

Presently, as though uneasy, even in the far-off Land of Nod, beneath those moveless, hungry, beautiful eyes, the young man stirred, and muttered something in his sleep. Swift and noiseless as a cat she leaped backward into the folded shadows; but he did not wake. Once more she came forward. With a stealthy movement she drew out a little pair of scissors from the bosom of her dress; then bending over, lifted, with the touch of a butterfly upon a flower, one of Roden's much-tossed curls. There was the sharp hiss of steel through hair, and the soft brown semicircle lay in the girl's palm. She lifted it to her lips with the gesture of one who, half starved, suddenly finds bread within his grasp; then turning, she stole out again, even as she had entered.

V.

Roden was not able to leave the house for many days. During this time Virginia waited upon him, sang to him, brought into service her every power of amusement.

She coaxed her perverse "mammy" to teach her new darky songs by reading endless chapters in the Bible. All her spare time was spent in setting them to appropriate accompaniments. She would sit and recount absurd anecdotes to him by the hour in her slow, sweet monotone, as unsuggestive of anything humorous as can well be imagined. Sometimes she fetched her spinning-wheel and spun as she talked. He felt vexed with himself that he could not sketch her as she sat plying the dull blue thread with her nimble fingers. Her homespun dress dropped naturally into those broad, generous folds beloved of sculptors. She had a clear, placid profile, which always found shadows sufficiently willing to serve as background for its pale beauty. Her head was noble in its contours, and as graceful in its startled, listening movements as that of a stag. Roden did make several attempts to fix her upon paper, but ended always with a contemptuous exclamation and a hurried, clever drawing of a steeple-chase, or Bonnibel, or some other equally horsy subject.

One day he happened to mention that as a lad he had played tolerably well on the violin. Virginia rose at once, saying that she thought there was one in the attic.

She took a candle, and went up the little corkscrew staircase that led into the roof of the house — a dark, dusty, cavernous place, smelling of mould and old books. There were many hair-covered trunks studded with brass nails, heaps of old saddles and harness, fire-dogs, brass and iron, a disused loom.

The corners of the room were veiled in a thick and rustling obscurity, suggestive of parchment and rats. Onions and red peppers adorned the ceiling.

Virginia set down the candle on one of the moth-eaten trunks, and lifted the lid of a second.

A fine cloud of little white particles flew out into her face, as impalpable, as easy of escape, as impossible to recapture, as the contents of Pandora's box. The girl thrust in her long brown arm, and drew out a bunch of white ostrich feathers.

They were shedding their delicate moth-nibbled filaments like snow upon her dark gown and the bare floor of the attic. She drew them caressingly through her fingers as though in pity; it seemed to her sad that things so charming should have so common a fate. She then stooped, and after a little searching drew out the violin.

She was about to shut down the lid of the trunk when something caught her eye—a bunch of cherry-colored ribbon, which burst from beneath a mass of moth-eaten gray fur, like a sudden flame from covering ashes.

She reached down and pulled it out; but lo! it was not only a knot of ribbons; something more followed—a sleeve of heavy antique silk, stiffly brocaded in red and gold flowers on a cream-hued ground. Then came more ribbons, a mass of fine lace, a scarlet petticoat. The girl put down the violin, held up this relic of the Old Dominion, and shook it out somewhat contemptuously. A little parcel fell from the musty skirt—a pair of slippers with high red heels and little red rosettes. As she looked, a sudden change came over the girl's face, a sudden flash of resolve, a quick suffusion of bright color. She seized the little shoes, bundled them again into the dress, and drew her own homespun skirt over the whole. Then, tucking the violin under her arm and lifting the candle, she ran at a perilously hurried pace down the contorted stair-way and into her own room.

She closed and locked the door, laid the dress and violin on the bed, and still standing up, pulled and tugged at one of her heavy shoes until it came off in her hand, discovering one of her shapely feet in its blue yarn stocking. But, alas! Virginia present could not get her foot into the slipper of Virginia past. She sat down on the edge of the bed in mortified vanquishment, and turned the pretty, absurd thing about in her strong hand. Then once more she tried to put it on. She found that by squeezing her toes into the toe of the slipper she could manage to walk, as there was no restraint at the back of the foot. She then lifted and put on the dress. It would not meet by several inches about her splendid young bosom, and the waist gaped at her derisively from the little mahogany-framed mirror. She was, however, determined. She hid these defects as best she might, by snipping away bunches of the cherry-colored ribbon here and there, and pinning them in reckless profusion above the gap in the bodice. My lady of the time of George the Third must have been shorter than this damsel of the first year of President Cleveland's administration. The stiff, flowered skirts stopped short at least three inches above her instep. Virginia had fortunately very commendable ankles, and peeping thus from the mass of mould-stained red and yellow frillings, they looked as sleek and trim as the neck of a bluebird peeping from autumnal foliage.

She tilted the little glass forward by means of one of her discarded shoes thrust behind it, and darted a shamefaced glance at her transformed self. Bravo! bravo! Miss Herrick! You are worthy of that famous name. So hath Abbey oft drawn Julia, plenteous in her shining skirts and tresses, beribboned, beautiful. Ah! what eyes! what lips! what an exquisite expression, half of self-conceit, half of timid uncertainty! What a throat for a dove to envy, supporting the face kissed brown by the sun, like an orchid whose stem is fairer than its flower! Snood up that banner of golden hair, my good Virginia; twist it about with the string of little shells you yourself gathered last summer; make yourself as lovely as possible, my little fawn, for the sacrifice. The gods have demanded it from time immemorial — a band of fair maidens every year to appease the Minotaur Despair. Good-by, Virginia; good-by; good-by. Never again will that dim green glass reflect such looks from you. Do not forget the violin. Was it not for him that you went to fetch it? Is it not for him that you have forced your strong young body into the curveless dress of 1761? Is it not all for him? And even unto the end will it not be for him?

Roden, conscious only of her presence by the unusual rustling of her skirts, looked up questioningly. When he saw her, who she was, he started to his feet, his lips parting in an expression of utter amaze. It was as though one of the bepowdered Caryston dames had stepped from her massive gilt frame in the hall without and confronted him. He could say nothing but her name, in varied tones of astonishment, inquiry, and approval.

She stood before him on her high heels as uncertain as a child learning to walk, smoothing out the much-creased folds of her gay attire with restless, nervous fingers, the stringless violin in her other hand. "I—I—I look a awful fool—don't I?" she said, laughing not very merrily. "I—feel 's 'f I'd sorter got roots to my feet in these shoes." She thrust out one foot, in its incongruity of yarn stocking and Louis Quinze slipper, tilted it to one side, and regarded it in apparent absorption.

Roden was only thinking what a charming picture she made tricked out in all this red and gold of other days. She stood there before him like a beautiful present, clad in the garments of a past as beautiful. He felt a strange sensation of having stepped back into the time of Henry Esmond and the Virginians. He glanced down at his wrists, half expecting to see lace ruffles spring to adorn them, under the magic of the hour.

"You pretty child!" he said at last, "what on earth made you think of getting yourself up in this style?" But he knew that she was more than pretty. He would have liked to tell her so, only he was always very careful what he said to this little Virginian; and florid compliments, though perfectly adapted to the period of her costume, would smack of the familiar when considered under the lights of the nineteenth century.

He wondered at the radiance in her suddenly lifted face. How could he know that at last the so often asked question nearest to her heart was answered, and answered by him? He thought her pretty!

"I brought you the violin," she said, turning away with an effort. "I reckon I'd better go 'n' take off these things. They cert'n'y do look foolish—don't they?"

"No, don't," said Róden. "You ought to humor an invalid, you know. You are so awfully nice to look at in that queer old gown."

Dimples that he had never before seen, just born of joy, stole in and out about the corners of the girl's red lips. She was more even than beautiful; she was enchanting. How ever had she come by all those old-time airs and movements? Had she perchance imbibed the spirit of the past with the air of the old house where she had always lived? Did some of those old *grandes dames* lean from the walls at night to teach her that subtle, upward carriage of the head?

He forgot all about the violin, and stood looking at her in wondering absorption.

"I—I've got a new song for you," she said, presently, in a low voice. She seated herself sidewise at the piano, as though diffident of the furbelows that composed the back of her novel attire, striking at the same time noiseless chords with her left hand.

"You said you liked Scotch songs. I found this one in a old book that b'longed to my mother. She was Scotch. Mus' I sing it?"

"Please do," said Roden.

Thus encouraged, she sang to him in the following words:

"I hae a curl, a bricht brown curl,
  A bonny, bonny curl o' hair,
 An' close to my heart it nestles warm,
  But its brithers dinna ken it's there.

"I stole my curl, my silk-saft curl,
  My bonny, bonny curl o' hair,
 An' a' the nicht it sleeps upon my heart,
  But its master doesna ken it's there.

"O bricht, bricht curl! O luvely, luvely curl!
   O curl o' my bonny, bonny dear!
 I wad that again ye waur shinin' on his head,
   But I wad that his head waur here!"

Now although Roden had often before heard her sing, he was conscious of a sound in her voice to-night which was utterly new to him—a sound so marvellous, so altogether exquisite, so melting sweet, that he was almost afraid the beating of his heart would prevent some of its beauty from reaching him. There was in it a divine fulness which he had never before heard in a human voice. It was like the sea on summer nights. It was like the distant wind in many leaves. It was like the eternal complaint of the voices of the fields on April noons. It filled him with a sense of peace and unrest at the same time. It thrilled him and possessed him utterly. Blind that he was, however, no faintest inkling of what had produced this divine result came to his mind. He was touched, but touched only as he would have been by any other voice as perfect.

"My dear little girl," he said, bending over and kissing her smooth brow with one of his rash impulses, "we must see what can be done with that voice. I am thinking that you will add to the honor of your name some day, Miss Herrick."

She started to her feet. It was as though her very heart's blood had risen to meet his lips. A delicate, vivid rose-color dyed all her brow and temples. "How do you mean?—how do you mean?" she said, in a rough, shaken whisper, holding both hands against her heart as though afraid it would leap from her body.

"Never mind what I mean just now," he said, with the smile of a wiseacre; "and, Virginia, since you have sung that song so charmingly, I am sure that you will be glad for me about something which I am going to tell you."

Glad? Was she not always glad for anything which gave him joy? Had she not read her eyes almost sightless, night after night, in mastering that strange horse lore which would enable her to help him in his enterprises? She came nearer, in bright expectancy; lifted her face to meet his looks and words.

"Yes," she said; "please tell me. I know I'll be glad—I cert'n'y will."

"I am engaged to be married," he told her. "I am engaged to be married to Miss Mary Erroll, and—I want you to be the first to congratulate me, Virginia."

He could recall nothing afterwards but the swift withdrawing of her hands from his. He could not even remember how she had left the room. She seemed to vanish as though in reality she had been but a wraith summoned up by fancy from days long fled.

But Virginia? Ah, Virginia! Out, out, out into the night she sped on supple, unshod feet. She had torn off those queer little parodies of shoes at the hall door, and held them now mechanically to her breast as she ran.

The air, redolent with peach-blossoms and hyacinths just born, rushed to meet her from the dark jaws of the east, as though some leviathan should breathe with a sweet breath upon the night May earth. There was no moon in the lustrous blue-gray of the heavens, but the stars seemed trying to atone for her absence by their multitudinous shining.

As Virginia dashed on past a clump of box-bushes, her skirts brushing the stiff leaves set them rattling, and woke the nested birds to querulous complaints. Her feet were wet with the night grasses, and bruised with the pebbles of the carriage-drive. She reached the lawn gate, opened it, and rushed through. On, on, across a field of grass, close-cropped by the not fastidious sheep, who, warmly folded on a neighboring hill-side, still nibbled drowsily between their slumbers such luscious blades as were within their reach.

She came at last to a little enclosure set about with evergreens and almost knee-deep in withered grass. Her eyes, grown accustomed to the wan light, could make out two little hillocks, as it were, formed within by heaped-up earth, and clasped by the tangled herbage. Underneath their sometime verdant rises slept the first twain who in Virginia bore the name of Caryston. Side by side, so had they lain, in death together as in life they had been. Virginia knew well this their self-chosen resting-place. Here on summer afternoons would she come to knit. Here she always brought the first spring flowers, and here she had always placed boughs of white and purple lilacs every day while they lasted. She had dreamed and wondered and enjoyed here, and here she came to suffer, as from some subtle instinct a man turns to his childhood's home to die.

Just outside the wicket gate the daffodils were all in plenteous blossom, as though day, for once relenting, had dropped an armful of gold into the lap of night. On a locust-tree near by a mocking-bird trilled and warbled. She cast herself face down upon one of the graves, clasping it about with her bare arms, as one clasps a proven friend in time of trouble. She had spoken no word as yet. She suffered as keenly, as dumbly, as any creature, wild or tame, to whom there is no soul. But all at once a cry broke from her, then over and over again, "O my God! O my God! O my God!"

The sobbing piteousness of this desolate prayer as it tore its way from the depths of her wild heart—who shall write of it? Not I—not I—even if I could. She was a savage; she suffered like a savage. Will any say there was no justice in it? It is something, is it not, to be capable of passion such as that? She suffered beyond most people, men and women, it is true; but was she not in that much blessed above them?

She lay there until the dawn looked whitely above the eastern hills upon the waking earth. In her quaint old dress one might have thought her the tortured ghost of the woman who had so long slept in peace below the grass-hidden mound. She staggered, when at last she rose to her feet, and fell for a moment upon her knees. There was a sense of vagueness that possessed her. She did not seem to care now, somehow. She wondered if they would be married at the little church in the neighborhood, and if they would let her come. She thought *he* would. She thought that she would not mind much seeing it. Of course they would live here. She would see them together every day. Well, what of that? She was surprised in a dull way that it did not affect her more. Then she remembered that she had not made any bread for him, such as he liked, the night before.

Well, it was a pity; but it was too late; it wouldn't have time to rise now. She must think of something else. Morning came on apace, clad all in translucent beryl-colored robes, and brow-bound with gold and with scarlet.

The birds were waking and chattering, as women chatter over their morning toilets. Some more hyacinths had bloomed in the night, and there was a great clump of iris, that she had not noticed the day before, on the hill-top. A cardinal-bird, sweeping downward like a flame fallen from some celestial fire, made his morning bath in the hollow of a tulip-tree leaf —a relic of vanished winter filled by kindly spring with fragrant rain.

As she neared the lawn gate she saw some one leaning over it. A swart, red-kerchiefed figure, clad in a dress whose stripes of blue and white circled her large body as its hoops a barrel. It was Aunt Tishy. She pushed upon the gate, jamming her stout proportions uncomfortably in her haste to reach the girl.

"Gord! Miss Faginia, whar *is* you ben? An' gret day in de mawnin! what dat you got on, anyhow? Gord! Gord! ef de chile ain' jes ez wet 's 'f she'd ben caught in de Red Sea wid Phario. Honey, whar *is* you ben, in the name o' Gord? Tell yo' mammy. Is you been see a harnt? What de matter wid my baby? Gord! Gord! dem eyes sutney *is* ben look on suppn dradeful. Po' lamb! po' lamb! Look at dem little foots, an' de stockin's all war offen 'em same as de rats dun neaw 'em. Ain' yo' gwine tell yo' mammy, my lady-bug? Come 'long so. Mammy kin 'mos' kyar yo' ter de house."

Virginia submitted listlessly to the old black's blandishments. She was not sorry to have Aunt Tishy's massive arm about her. Her feet ached and smarted; there was a sharp pain in her side when she drew her breath, and that dreadful feeling of being a thing just born, a creature who had no past, still held her in its numbing grasp.

Aunt Tishy took her into the big kitchen—an out-house consisting of one room, and a fireplace in which one might have roasted a whole ox. It was lined on two sides with great smoke-darkened pine presses. The other walls and the ceiling had once been white, but were now stained the color of a half-seasoned meerschaum pipe. The two windows had casements with diamond-shaped panes of dingy glass set in lead. Enormous deal tables stood here and there. From the surrounding gloom came the glimmer of brightly polished tin, as brilliant in its effect as the glint of a negro's teeth from the dusk of his face.

Aunt Tishy, having seated her nursling in an old wooden rocking-chair, dragged a basket of chips and shavings from the capacious ingle-nook, and set about making the

"I GWINE TAKE DAT DAR OUTLANDISH THING OFFEN YO', HONEY."

fire. She first scooped away the yet warm ashes of yesterday with her shapely yellow-palmed hands. Negroes generally have well-formed hands and remarkably pretty finger-nails. Then she began laying a little foundation of shavings and lightwood splinters; here and there she stuck a broad locust-chip. When these preparations were all completed she went out to "fotch a light," she said, assuring Virginia of her speedy return.

In a few moments she was back, carrying a handful of live coals in her naked palm, having first sprinkled a few ashes over it for protection. With these she kindled the fire, which soon made a busy clamor in the hollow throat of the old chimney.

Once more she disappeared, returning with a bundle of things in her arms: a big shawl, Virginia's shoes and stockings, and her homespun dress.

"I gwine take dat dar outlandish thing offen yo', honey," she announced, seat-ing herself on the pine floor in front of the girl, and beginning to draw off her torn stockings. "I gwine mek yo' put on yo' own frawk 'fo' dey sees yo' in d' house. Marse Gawge he ain' knowin' nuttin' 'bout yo' bein' out all night. I 'mos' skeered to deaf 'bout yo', but I ain' seh nuttin' to *naw*body, 'case I didn't think my honey gwine g'way fur good." She took the little cold bare feet into her cushiony palms and rubbed them softly. Every now and then she bent down her gayly turbaned head and blew with warm breath upon them after the negro fashion of ministering to any frozen thing, from a bit of bread to a young "squawb."

"Yo' barf's all rade-y in de house," Aunt Tishy continued, as she knelt up and began unfastening the ribbons from the front of the old-time garment the girl had donned in a mood so different.

"Gord! honey," she said, as the pins accumulated in her capacious mouth, "in de name o' sense what dun persess yo' tuh put on dis hyah thing? Name o' Gord! *who* ever see sich a thing *any*how?" She held it up with much of the contempt with which Virginia had at first regarded it, tossing it finally into the chip-basket.

Virginia said nothing from first to last. She was almost sure that she was dreaming, and would soon awake.

"My sakes 'live!" chuckled Aunt Tishy, as she hooked the homespun dress about the girl's waist, "wouldn' I 'a' thanked Gordamighty ef yo'd 'a' ben dis good when yo' wuz leetle, honey? Mk, mh-*mph!*"

(This final ejaculation I find impossible to describe with pen and ink.)

When she had completely altered her charge's appearance, replaiting her dishevelled hair, and unwinding from its tangled meshes the little chain of white and red sea-shells, Aunt Tishy took her by the hand and led her across the side lawn to the house.

"Now yo' kin dress comfbul," she told her, "an' jess mek' yo'se'f easy, my lamb. Tishy she ain' gwine seh nuttin' tuh *naw-bode-y*."

Virginia tried to smile upon her. Something stiff at the corners of her mouth seemed to prevent her. She turned, lifting one hand to her cheek, and went into the yet quiet house.

VI.

Roden wondered a good deal during such moments as his thoughts reverted not to his ladylove, concerning Virginia's recent neglect of him. Popocatepetl was his attendant now at meals, dried his newspapers, and gambolled for his amusement. Virginia had come to him on the afternoon of the day following that upon which he had announced to her his engagement, and had said she "didn' know what took her las' night. She cert'n'y was glad he was so happy. He mus' please scuse her 'f she'd ben unperlite. She cert'n'y was glad." But Roden missed her very much. Besides, he wished exceedingly to hear her sing again. He wanted to be quite sure that he had not deluded himself in regard to the possibilities contained in her sonorous voice.

Virginia continued to be very economical of her presence, however, and three days afterwards he was summoned to New York by telegraph to attend the bedside of an ailing thorough-bred.

Virginia did not come to tell him good-by. He thought it strange at the moment, but did not have time to ponder over it subsequently. She, in the mean time, kneeling behind the "slats" of her bedroom window-blinds, watched the little Canadian fishing-wagon as it drove away, with Popocatepetl proudly installed on the back seat. She held something crushed against her breast—an old Trinity College boating-cap which belonged to Roden. She knelt there for full a half-hour after the last grinding of the cart-wheels on the carriage-drive. No tears rose to soothe the burning in her eyes. She had not wept since that night spent by those lonely graves. At last she rose and went over beside the fire. The day was unusually raw for the season of the year.

Rebellious robins chattered on the eaves. A fitful wind swept rudely over the fields. Virginia, with unseeing eyes on the low-smouldering fire, caressed the bit of blue cloth in her hands with absent, slow-moving fingers. Anon she lifted and examined it closely. It seemed to her that the lion on the coat of arms might have been better done. She remembered an old print of Daniel in the lions' den which was in the big family Bible. Therein the king of beasts was, she thought, far more ably depicted. This lion had an inane expression, owing probably to the two black dots which stood for his fierce eyes, a paucity of mane, and a superfluity of tail which struck her as undignified. Suddenly she burst out laughing. Peal after peal of the merry, staccato sound rang through the winding passageways above, and echoed down into the lower halls; ripple upon ripple of wild merriment; a rush, an abandonment of jollity, in which she had not indulged for many a day. She tried in vain to stop. She could not. That little oblong lion with his much-curled tail was too much for her. Ha! ha! Oh, how funny — how funny it was! and how she enjoyed a good laugh! And was it not far, far better to laugh than to cry? Oh, that funny, funny, funny little beast! How merry he made her, how jolly, how care-free, once more!

A voice rang out suddenly, calling her name: "Faginia! O-o-o-o Faginia! O-o-o-o Faginia!"

Startled into sudden gravity, she slipped the cap into the breast of her brown stuff gown, and went to the door.

"That you, father?"

"Yase, 'tis. What 'n th' name o' goodness 'r' you hyahhyahin' 'bout up thar all by yo'self? Howsomdever, the beauty of the question air, thar's a young lady down here as wants ter see you, an' I'd never 'a' knowed yo' was in the house ef yo' hadn' been goin' on like a wil'-cat with the stomach-ache."

"Who is it?" said Virginia.

Back came the name in strident unmistakable syllables, "Miss—Ma-ry—Er-roll."

There was a second's pause.

"I'll be down in a minute," Virginia called back.

Miss Mary Erroll was walking up and down the "front hall" in her Quorn-cloth habit, whistling softly to herself. Her short riding-skirt needed no holding up to enable her to move comfortably, and her hands were clasped behind her about her hunting-crop.

Virginia, coming slowly down the many convolutions of the broad stair-way, noticed the dark sheen of the thick braid folded away under the smart little hat, the glimpse of fair cheek and throat, the thorough-bred lines of the slight figure.

"Mornin'," she said, briefly.

Miss Erroll stopped in the midst of an intricate aria, unbent her red lips, and held out her hand in its loose dog-skin glove:

evidently she intended to ignore the unpleasantness of their last interview.

"I came to Caryston for two reasons," she announced, cheerily. "First, to give your father a message which Mr. Roden left with me. Secondly, to bring you something, Miss Virginia. I believe you like dogs?"

"Some dawgs," said Virginia, speaking in a dull, even tone.

Miss Erroll, nothing daunted, led the way to the library; she pulled off the wrappings from about a wicker basket, and lifted out a sturdy mastiff pup, who, supported across the palm of his whilom mistress's fair hand, made ungainly motions with his great paws, as though trying to swim.

"Won't you take him, Miss Virginia? We have so many dogs at home, it would be a real kindness."

"Most likely my father 'd like to have him," said Virginia. "I don't have much time ter 'tend ter dawgs. I'm much obliged ter you, though."

Miss Erroll, thus rebuffed, set down the little mastiff on the floor, and pushed it with the toe of her riding-boot. One of the characteristics of this young woman was an insatiate desire for the good-will of every one. It was weak, no doubt; but, as the celebrated saying hath it, the weakness was very strong. Somehow it made Mary uncomfortable to think that the overseer's daughter, humble though her position was, should not succumb to the charm which she chose to exert for her benefit.

The unconscious little peace-offering in the mean time was making abortive efforts to peer into every object out of his reach which the room contained.

A sudden revulsion of feeling came over Virginia, a sense of unnecessary rudeness, and of the uselessness of it all.

"I—I'll take him, thank you," she said, stooping and lifting the puppy into her capable young embrace. "I'm mighty glad to have him. He cert'n'y is pretty."

Poor Virginia! She felt the baldness of these phrases without knowing how to remedy them. "He cert'n'y is cunnin'," she added.

Mary was much relieved. "I thought you would like him," she said. "I have named him 'Mumbo,' after one of his ancestors. If you don't like the name, please be sure to change it."

"Oh, I like it!" said Virginia. "I couldn't give him a better one to save my life. I kyarn't never scarsely think o' names fur the critters on th' farm. Does he know it yet?"

"Oh no!" Miss Erroll assured her.— "You'll have to teach him that."

She looked down intently at one of her gloves, and began to unbutton it. "I suppose you have heard of my engagement?" she said, without looking up.

Yes, Virginia had heard of it. She said so in an even monotone which had in it no suggestions either of approval or disapproval. She was astonished to feel Miss Erroll's hand on her arm.

"Miss Virginia," said that young lady, with a sweet and whole-souled blush, " I'm going to ask you to do me a tremendous favor. I — I would like so much to see Jack's — Mr. Roden's room just as he left it, don't you know — with his boots and coats and whips lying about. I don't want your father or any of the servants to know, because they would think me crazy; but I'm sure you'll understand."

Virginia led the way without a word. The mastiff pup made playfully affectionate dabs at her round chin with his rose-leaf tongue. Roden's bedroom was on the ground-floor. He did not occupy the majestically gloomy apartment in which his first night at Caryston had been spent. This room was in the east wing of the house, plentifully perforated with small casements, and panelled from floor to ceiling. This panelling had all been painted white, and the result of the heavy coatings, renewed from time to time, was a rich, ivory-like smoothness of tint and tone. A little single iron bedstead stood in one corner of the room, between two windows. There were some capital old sporting prints upon the walls, numberless hunting-crops and riding-canes stacked on the high mantle, spurs, gloves, tobacco-bags, cartridges, and what not heaped pell-mell on tables and chairs, about twenty pairs of boots and shoes ranged along one side of the room, some on and some not on trees. Garments of divers kind were pitched recklessly about. It is perhaps needless to say, after the foregoing description, that confusion reigned supreme.

Miss Erroll, at first shyly conscious of Virginia's presence, soon began to move about after her usual airy fashion. She lifted the brier-wood pipe, so often smoked in Virginia's presence, and pressed her lips playfully to its glossy bowl.

"Aren't women geese, Miss Virginia,

when they care for any one?" she said, turning to laugh at the girl over her graceful shoulder.

She was entirely at her ease now, and went about from object to object, touching some and merely looking at others, with a little conscious air of possession which was like the turning of a rusty knife in the girl's heart. She tossed an old shooting-coat from the bed's foot to a chair, remarking, as she did so, "What careless creatures the best of men are! I shall have to give Master Jack a lesson in the old proverb concerning places and things—when—when I am Mrs. Jack!" she ended, merrily.

Turning over some things on a table near one of the windows she came across an old-fashioned netted purse of red silk, with steel rings and tassels—the purse Virginia had netted for him during such odd moments as she could steal from her many occupations. She watched Miss Erroll now with hungry eyes, the eyes of a wounded lioness who watches, helpless, the taking away of one of her cubs. Her heart beat against her homespun bodice with short, quick throbs. She stooped and set the struggling puppy upon the floor. It seemed to her as though she had been holding fire in her arms.

"Oh, this is so pretty!" said unconscious Mary. "This is so very quaint and pretty! I must have it. Of course he'd give it me. I'm just going to take it without saying by your leave;" and with that she slipped it in the pocket of her habit.

Virginia shut her eyes for a moment, dizzy with pain and anger; but the red light which seemed to surround and envelop her when she did so made her fainter than ever. She lifted her dark lids and stared out at the blank strip of sky above the box-bushes outside the window, vacantly, unseeingly.

She had no distinct recollection of the remainder of Miss Erroll's visit. That one fact concerning the taking away of the purse which Roden had promised to keep always alone remained distinctly in her mind. She had tried honestly to overcome the all-powerful, unreasoning dislike of Miss Mary Erroll, and the result had been worse than if it had not been tried. The discordant, insistent yapping of the mastiff pup irritated her almost beyond endurance. He seemed bent on intruding upon her his regret for the departure of his former mistress.

As she went wearily into her father's work-room, and sat down to her spinning-wheel, she heard his voice at the window calling her.

"Well?" she said, listlessly.

"'Pears to me," said he, jocosely, "as having rained, it air cert'n'y pourin'. Heah's Joe Scott come ter bring yo' them jorhnny-jump-ups he sez as he promised yo'."

She got violently to her feet, upsetting the wheel and tearing her skirt against a projecting nail as she hastened to the window. "Tell him I'm sick," she said. "Tell him I'm in bade. I ain't a-goin' ter see him; that's flat. If needs be, tell him so."

But Mr. Joseph Scott had already entered the room. He was a person of sinuous, snake-like presence, and seemed capable of shedding his complete attire by means of one deft wriggle. His neck rose from a turn-down celluloid collar, after the fashion of the neck of "Alice in Wonderland," after she had partaken of the cake which caused her to exclaim, "Curiouser, and curiouser!" His long locks, of a vague, smoky tint, exuded an unsavory smell of (I am ashamed to say) rancid pomatum. He wore a threadbare summer overcoat, though in his case the "over" was a decided misnomer, as there was nothing under it but an unbleached cotton shirt, and a sporting vest which had evidently belonged to some Briton. His necktie would have put an October forest to the blush. His mud-colored trousers were pulled down outside of his great cowhide boots, which presented their very apparent tops in a ridgy circle beneath the stuff of his trousers.

A strangling sense of loathing and revolt rose in Virginia's throat. She felt as though she would indeed suffocate beneath that terrible combination of smell and vulgarity. She leaned far out of the window, and spoke to him without turning her head.

"Mornin'," she said, curtly. "P'r'aps you heard me tell father I was sick."

"Lor'! air you?" said Mr. Scott. "I cert'n'y am sawry. Here's them jorhnny-jump-ups I hearn you seh ez how you wanted."

"Thank you," said Virginia, in a stifled voice. She still leaned out of the window, and the conversation flagged.

"Larse night," suddenly announced Mr. Scott, with spasmodic assertiveness, "Larse night a peeg-horg came down th' mounting and gneawed all pa's corn orf."

"He must 'a' had a mighty leetle crop,"

said Virginia from without the window. Her voice came back into the room softened by the purring air without.

"I'm tawkin' 'bout gyarden corn," said Mr. Scott, failing to appreciate the sarcasm.

Again a silence. The mastiff pup, diverted by the arrival of the new-comer, went sniffing about his redolent person.

"Ef he was a fox," thought Virginia, dryly, "'twouldn't take no houn's ter foller his scent. I could track him a week arterwards myself." Out aloud she said, "Air them roots or flowers you brought me?"

"Both," said Mr. Scott.

Another pause.

"The tarryfied fever's a-ragin' up ter Annesville," he announced, presently.

Virginia faced about for the first time. "Is it?" she asked. "Who's down?"

"Nigh all o' them Davises. The doctor says as how it's 'count o' their makin' fertilizer in their cellar."

"HE MUST 'A' HAD A MIGHTY LEETLE CROP."

"What?" said Virginia.

He repeated his assertion.

"Ef that's true," she said, slowly, "I ain' goin' to bother my head 'bout 'em; such fools oughter die."

(Be that as it may, she "bothered" herself enough to tramp on foot all the way to

Annesville, some eight miles, that very afternoon, and offer her services as sick-nurse. The house fortunately was under quarantine, and there was assistance enough.)

"But that ain' nothin' ter th' skyarlet-fever over the mounting," Mr. Scott pursued, in a tone whose threadbare lugubriousness revealed the morbid satisfaction which lined it. "That's fyar howlin'; an' they sez, moresomeover, ez how it can be kyard an' took from a little bit o' rag."

Old Herrick, who had come again to the window, was listening intently. "'S that so?" he said, finally. "Well, consequently were, the beauty of that question air, thar ain' much rag trade goin' on between that side o' th' mounting an' t'other. Hyeah! hyeah!"

"How can you laugh, father?" said the girl.

"Godamighty, gyrl! I ain' laufin' at the folks as is got the fever, but at them as ain't."

"They says as how it kin be kep' in a piece o' ribbon or sich fur over twenty year," pursued Mr. Scott, who, apparently not content with his own fragrance, continued from time to time to bury his long nose in the bunch of johnny-jump-ups which he still held.

"'S that so?" said old Herrick again. "I tell yo' what, darter, 'f that thar's true, yo'd better have them things ez th' las' Englisher's wife lef' up in th' attic burned up."

"Why?" said Mr. Scott, before Virginia could reply.

"'Case thar baby died o' th' red fever, and thar's some o' its belongin's up thar inter a cradle—some little odds an' eens ez they furgot ter take away with 'em in their trouble."

"Yo'd cert'n'y better burn 'em," said Mr. Scott, with knowing gloom. "I'd as soon sleep with a bar'l o' gunpowder over my hade."

"Well, seems to me ef there's danger

'n either, 'twouldn't be in th' gunpowder," said Miss Herrick, dryly, "seein' as it don' never blow down, an' yo'd be onder it."

"G'long, Miss Faginia!" exclaimed her not-to-be-rebuffed admirer. "Yo'd have yo' joke 'bout a dyin' minister!"

He left a half-hour afterwards, all unconscious of the seeds of disaster which he had sown, and the next day Roden returned from New York in excellent spirits. On the following Tuesday he went into the kitchen and had a private conference with Aunt Tishy, which resulted in his leaving it with pockets considerably lightened, and shoulders laden with the thanks and praise of its proprietress. He also confided in Virginia, and asked her assistance. He wished to give his bride-elect and her mother a little dinner — wouldn't Virginia help him? She was so very clever about such things. He knew if she would only help him that everything would be perfectly satisfactory. She promised, and he went off on Bonnibel to Windemere entirely content.

Miss Erroll drove her mother over to Caryston in a village-cart, and, as luck would have it, a sudden shower caught them about a quarter of a mile from the house. Mary, however, got the brunt of the shower, as she was driving, and had at once wrapped her mother in all available rugs and wraps.

Mrs. Erroll stepped out upon the front porch at Caryston with the ruffle at her throat, and a little damp, and the plumes in her bonnet somewhat limp; but Mary's dress of white wool was soaked through and through, and her hat a sodden mass of white lace and straw.

Roden relapsed at once into the agonies of alarm in which newly engaged men are apt to indulge when the health of their *fiancées* is called into question. He went again to Virginia, and overwhelmed her with instruction and entreaties. Miss Erroll was conducted to a bedroom bright with blue chintz and many wax-candles, and Virginia, having provided her with some of her own clothes, went off to dry the soaked garments. That, however, Roden would not hear of. It was too far to Windemere to send back for dry garments. Then Virginia must lend Miss Erroll one of her dresses.

Virginia had three dresses besides the one she wore. She brought them all in and laid them on the bed. Miss Mary, who had an artistic eye, chose a gown of garnet wool with plain round waist and short skirt. When she had turned it in a little at the throat, and fastened a bit of cambric, which Virginia brought her, kerchiefwise about her neck, she looked like a charming Cinderella who had resumed her humble attire to please her Prince. Mary's throat, however, could not stand the severe test of laceless exposure. It was too slender and long. Where Virginia's massive column of cream-hued flesh rose from the clasp of such a kerchief with infinite suggestions of mythical forests and Amazonian warriors, Miss Erroll announced that she looked "scraggy." She took up the bit of black velvet with its buckle of Scotch pebbles which she had worn about her throat when she arrived. But the wet stuff left dark stains on her fingers, and had assumed a cottony, lack-lustre hue. "If only I had a bit of velvet to go about my throat!" she said, regretfully. "I can't go down this way—I'm so indecently thin!" She laughed a little and sat down as in despair.

A sudden thought leaped hot in Virginia's breast. A bit of velvet? She had no velvet of any kind, but she knew where a piece was. A bit of dark-blue velvet ribbon, just such a bit as Miss Erroll wanted. True, it had been used to loop a baby's sleeve, but around that slender throat it would reach most amply.

"I—kin—get—you a piece," she heard herself saying.

Her voice sounded strange and disembodied to herself, as though it did not issue from her own lips. She thought that she to whom she spoke must start up with horror for the change. But no, she only smiled blandly, sweetly, with that faint suggestion of patronage which was as perceptible, though not as palatable, as the dash of bitter in orange marmalade.

"Thank you so much!" she said. "I shall quite suit myself then."

Virginia took a candle and went up into the attic, as ten days ago she had gone. The damp, dusty smell brought back to her that terrible memory as only a perfume can recall the past.

Her veins throbbed ever hotter and fiercer. Her time was come. Revenge was in her hands. What fever could be more virulent, more deadly, than the fever that dark-haired girl had set raging in her veins? What was the verse that she had read only last night to Aunt Tishy out of what the old negress called "de Holy Wud?" An eye for an eye, a tooth for a tooth. Joe Scott was not the only person she had ever heard speak of such a thing. It had simply served to recall it to her mind. Ha! ha! She had never liked Joe Scott before, and she had been very rude about those johnny-jump-ups. Poor Joe! She would thank him the very best she knew how when next she saw him. Poor Joe! good Joe! dear Joe! Yes, there it was, the pretty bassinet cradle, with its faded blue and pink ribbons. That little English baby had died full four years ago. She walked towards it, shielding the candle with one scooped hand from the playful assaults of the night wind. The cradle stood just in front of an old hair-covered chest. As she neared it, a consciousness of eyes regarding her came upon her. Ah! there they were. A rat, paralyzed for the moment by the sudden light, had paused on the edge of the old chest, and fixed her with his little, protruding, evil-looking eyes. She made a spasmodic, terrified movement with her hand, and he leaped down, his sleek, tight-skinned body striking the floor with a repulsive sound as of unsavorily nurtured corpulence. The girl turned with a strong, uncontrollable fit of shivering towards the cradle. It was rocking slowly back and forth in the uncertain light, its pink and blue ribbons fluttering with a ghostly and ill-timed gayety. A cry almost broke from between her gripped lips, but she remembered suddenly that the rat must have set it in motion when he leaped from the top of the chest. Setting the candle on the floor beside her, she stooped over and began lifting out the little sheets and blankets and bundles of linen and silk. One of those sudden noises which disturb sleep at night in an old house jarred through the room. She stuffed the things hastily back and looked behind her. Nothing there. But as her glance went round the room she saw before her, black, assertive, monstrous, the likeness of a huge cradle, cast by the candle against the whitewashed wall of the garret. Her heart beat with laboring, heavy thuds. If it were not quite so black, she thought, or if it had only been more the size of the real cradle; but its vast presence in the low-roofed room seemed like the presence of some presiding fate. She tore away her look from it by sheer force of will, found what she wanted, caught up the candle, and rushed headlong from the room.

Miss Erroll received her with the same sweet smile. "You were pretty long," she said. "I'm afraid I've given you a lot of trouble."

"No, none," said Virginia. She cleared her throat and repeated the words. They were indistinct at first, because of the dryness of her tongue and the roof of her mouth. She watched with hot, moveless eyes the slim fingers of Miss Erroll as she first crimped the curling bit of velvet between her fingers, with a deft, almost imperceptible movement, and forced the teeth of her little buckle through it.

"How damp it smells!" she said, as she lifted it to her throat to put it on; "just as if it had been stuffed away in some old attic."

Virginia's knees smote together. She put out her hand to steady herself, and sank heavily into a chair.

"'Tain't nuthin'—'tain't nuthin'," she said, roughly, as Mary ran to her side. "I'm better jess so. Don' tech me, please. An' please ter scuse me. I kyarn' bear no one to tech me when—when I'm like this."

Alas! alas! Virginia, when were you ever "like this" before, in the whole course of your seventeen years of strength and health and placid, if bovine, contentment?

The dinner, thanks to Virginia, was a success. Roden's wines were excellent.

They were going to ask Virginia to sing for them. Roden said he thought it would please her so much. After dinner Mrs. Erroll sat down to the piano, and the sweethearts wandered off into the "greenhouse," leaving open the door between the rooms. A rhomboid of pale yellow light from the candles on the dinner-table fell into the narrow, flower-crowded corridor, touching the great geranium-leaves into a soft distinctness, and showing here and there the flame-colored and snow-white glomes of blossom.

Roden, out of sight of Mrs. Erroll, had straightway put an arm about the supple waist of his betrothed, and one of her hands had found its way to his short curls with a movement as of long habit. As the slanting light from the room beyond caught the sheen of her delicate throat above its velvet ribbon, he bent his head and pressed down his lips upon it and upon the bit of velvet.

Virginia, by some strange coincidence or freak of fate, was at this moment crossing the lawn to put the mastiff pup into his kennel. Attracted by the unusual light in the greenhouse, she looked up. Looking up, she saw Roden as he stooped and kissed his sweetheart's throat. She gave a fierce broken cry, like an angered beast, and turning, ran with all her might into the house.

Poor Mrs. Erroll, summoning up musical ghosts from her maidenhood's *répertoire* on the old piano, thought that one of Roden's horses had gone mad and galloped through the room.

In the mean time Virginia, panting, wordless, seized Mary with one strong hand, and with the other tore off the velvet from about her neck. "I—I—I've read as how it was pizen; I jess remembered. Here's yo' buckle."

She rushed madly out again, and flinging herself upon the bare floor of her little bedroom, beat the hard boards with her hand and dragged at her loosened hair.

VII.

There is One who hath said that to Him belongeth vengeance. When His creatures take into their incapable grasp the javelins of His wrath it is generally with as impotent and baleful a result as when young Phaëton, seeking to guide the chariot of the sun, brought to himself despair, and scorched to cinders the unoffending earth. Thus was it with Virginia. With the nearness of her unbridled love and anger she had forever seamed as if with fire the fair world of her content. It seemed to her that space itself would be too narrow to hold her apart from such women as were good and true.

Just God! could it be that her sin was to be visited upon the being whom of all the world she loved best, because of whom that sin had been committed? Was Roden going to suffer, perhaps to die, in the stead of the woman she had sought to slay? He was not often at Caryston now; most of his days were spent with his betrothed. He did not notice the change which was stealing over Herrick's daughter. He had no time to wonder that she did not sing now at her spinning as once she had sung. He would not have paused to listen to her had she done so.

He was called away again to the North on the last of May, and on the day after his departure Aunt Tishy burst into Virginia's room with flour-covered hands. "Gord! Gord! honey," she said, tossing her blue-checked apron up and down with wild, savage gestures of dismay and grief, "what yuh think?—Marse Jack's sweetheart's dun got de rade fever, an' dey don' think as how she'll live."

Virginia stood and stared at her with eyes which saw nothing. Her face took on a ghastly greenish pallor. About her brow and mouth there stole a cold moisture. She opened her lips, and seemed to speak. Her lips framed the same words stupidly over and over again.

"Gord! honey," cried the old negress, seizing her, as she swayed backward as if about to fall, "is yuh gwine be sick yuhsef?"

Virginia pushed her away, walked steadily over to an old oak cupboard, took out a jug of whiskey, and drank from its green glass throat as she had seen men do. The stinging liquid filled her veins with a hot, false strength. She spoke quickly now, in a harsh tone, seizing the old nurse by the shoulders, and thrusting her white face, with its lambent, distended eyes, close to that of the terrified Aunt Tishy.

"When was she took? Who tol' yuh? Are yuh lyin'? Ef yuh're lyin' I'll curse yuh with such curses yuh won' be able to be still when yuh're dead. But yuh wouldn' lie tuh me, would yuh, mammy? You wouldn' lie to me to send me tuh hell in th' spirit 'fo' I was called there fur good. Yuh hear me? Why didn' yuh tell me befo'? Who's with her? Who's nursin' her? Put up my clo'es. I'm goin'—I'm goin' right now. God! Air yuh a-tryin' to hold me? Ha! ha! That's good — that cert'n'y is good. I'll make father larf at that when—when I come back. Why, you pore old thing, I could throw you outer that winder ef I tried. Well, don't cry. What a' you cryin' fur? God! God! God! have mercy on me!"

She fell upon her knees, wringing her hands and throwing backward her agonized face, as though with her uplooking, straining eyes she would pierce the very floor of heaven and behold that mercy for which she pleaded. Then she leaped again to her feet. All at once a calmness fell upon her. She resumed the old dull listlessness of some days past as though it had been a garment.

"I'm goin' to Mis' Erroll's," she said, quietly. "I wan' some clo'es. Send 'em; I ain't er-goin' tuh wait. Tell father."

Virginia, arrived at Windemere, went down the basement steps into the kitchen. The cook, a young mulatto woman named Lorinda, came forward to meet her on cautious, brown-yarn toes.

"Miss Mary's a-dyin'," she announced, in a sepulchral whisper. "De doctor seh ez how she kyarn' live nohow. She's jess ez rade ez a tomarker fum hade tuh foots. An' she's jess pintly 'stracted. Yuh never heah sich screechin' an' tuh-doin' in all yuh life."

"Kin I see Mis' Erroll?" Virginia said, shortly. She sat down on an upturned half-barrel near the door, and leaned with her forehead in her locked palms. Lorinda, rebuffed but obliging, went to see. Virginia was not surprised when she returned shortly, followed by Mrs. Erroll herself. Her heart would never quicken its beat again for anything this side of torment, she thought. Poor, erring, repentant, suffering little savage, what are you enduring now if it be not torment?

Mrs. Erroll, nervous and hysterical, took the girl's hands in hers, and scarcely knowing what she did, bent forward and kissed her cheek. Virginia started back with a harsh cry, which was born and died in her throat.

"Poor child!" Mrs. Erroll said, humbly. "I beg your pardon. But if you feared contagion you ought not to have come here."

"'Tain't that—'tain't that," said Virginia. "Don' min' me; I'm queer like sometimes. I didn' mean nuthin'. Ev'ybordy in this neighborhood 'll tell yo' I'm a good nurse. I've come to he'p yo'. I've come to take kyar of her. I've come to *make* her live!"

She lifted one arm with a gesture of command almost threatening. The next moment it dropped heavily to her side. The old dull look crept like a shadow over the momentary animation of her face. "They'll tell yo' I'm a good nurse," she said, in her slow monotone.

Mrs. Erroll was only too thankful for the proffered services. She had no assistance from the whites in the neighborhood; indeed, all of the neighboring families had left for the Virginia Springs.

Virginia, after removing her shoes, went at once to the sick-room. As her eyes fell upon the flushed face on the pillow it was as if every drop of blood in her body turned first to fire and then to ice.

She stood with her hands against her breast and looked down at her own work. The beautiful dark tresses, formerly so smoothly braided about the small head, now ever turning from side to side as though in search of rest which it found not, were tangled and matted until no trace of their former lustre remained; the red lips, ever moving, gave forth wild, incoherent cries and mutterings.

About the slender throat coiled the wraith of a dark-blue velvet ribbon.

"Take it off, take it off," whispered Virginia. "She kyarn' git well while that's there—she kyarn'." Reason came back to her with a sudden rush, and she knew that only her mind's eye saw the velvet ribbon.

She then took her place by the bedside, from which she did not move to eat or sleep for twelve days and nights. They brought her bouillon and made her drink it under penalty of being turned from the room. For twelve times four-and-twenty hours she listened to those senseless ravings. She was mistaken in turn by the sick girl for her mother, for some of her school-room friends, for Roden. Mary would sometimes put up both narrow, fever-wasted hands to her little throat, and cry out that she was choking—that Virginia had brought her a band of fire and locked it about her throat. By what strange coincidence such a fancy should have possessed her who shall say?

Thus they went together, those two, through the Valley of the Shadow—the all but murdered, the almost murderess—and she who had sought to slay brought back to life.

Roden, detained by some business complication in New York, heard nothing of his sweetheart's illness until telegraphed for on the day of the crisis. It was just the balance of a mote in sunshine between life and death. Life brought the mote that won. They told him he must thank Virginia. They had all thanked her, and blessed her, with thanks and blessings which burned her guilty soul with twice the fire of red-hot maledictions. That they should bless her whom God had cursed! Ah, God, she prayed not! She would but know if God himself wept not because of the sad mockery.

A wild thought came to her with healing in its wings, as when a blade of grass forces its way between the stones in a prisoner's cell. She had read of atonement: might she not atone?

Perhaps God would let her buy forgiveness with her life. Why had she not taken the fever; or was this fever now which rioted through her veins? She was walking homeward with her shoes slung across her shoulders. The grass felt cool and damp against her bare feet. Would it not wither where she trod? She looked backward over her shoulder with a laugh. It seemed to her that her footprints would be set as with fire across that lush June field.

Then came a curse upon her eyes. For her the earth lost all its summer green; the heavens above her bent not bluely down to meet the blue horizon. The birds ceased singing, and echoed her mirthless laugh; all nature took it up—a monstrous harmony of jovial sounds. At what were they making merry, these creatures large and small—the crickets, the wild birds, the many voices of field and forest, of air and water?

Was it at her they laughed? Did they jeer at her because she had lost her soul? Ah, for the cool green to look upon! Ah, that its blue would return to the lurid heavens! The curse of blood was upon her. Because of it she looked on all things as through a scarlet veil. Red was the vault above her; red the far-reaching line of well-loved hills; red, red, the whirling earth.

Virginia did not die. A week after her recovery she sent and asked if Roden would come to her father's room; she wished to speak with him.

He went most willingly, having never felt as though he had sufficiently thanked her for what she had done for one who was to him as the life in his veins.

As he entered the room, in spite of all his self-control he could not restrain a slight start. Was this Virginia Herrick? —this snow maiden with eyes of fire, and tangled hair that seemed to flame about her white face as though it would consume it?—this fragile, wasted, piteous memory of a woman? She was as poor a likeness of her former self as a sketch in white chalk would be of one of Fortuny's sunlit glares of canvas.

He came and stood beside her, wordless, and then put one of his strong brown hands kindly on her hair.

"Wait," she said, drawing herself away from him—" wait."

"Ah, Miss Virginia," he said, in his breezy, gentle voice, "we will soon have you out of this. You won't know yourself in two weeks."

"Wait," she said, her great eyes burning into his.

"My poor little girl," he said, almost with tenderness, "I am afraid you have overestimated your strength. You had better let me go now. I will come to-morrow whenever you send for me."

"Wait," she said a fourth time, in that strange, still voice.

He had a horrified doubt in regard to her reason as he took the chair to which she pointed and sat down facing her.

"Well," he said, with an assumption of gayety which he was far from feeling, "what is it? Am I to be scolded for anything?"

"Do you believe in torment?" said the girl. She kept her hollow, stirless eyes on his. There was an absence of movement about her almost oppressive. She seemed not even to breathe.

"My dear child," said Roden, nervously, "do choose a more cheerful subject. Really, you know, it isn't good for you to be morbid now. Let's talk of something jolly and pleasant. Don't you want to hear how the mokes are coming along? And Bonnibel, poor old girl! I'm afraid her feelings will be awfully hurt when I tell her you didn't ask after her."

"I s'pose ev'ybordy bleeves in torment that has felt it," said the girl. She had not moved in anywise. Her deep, still eyes yet rested on his face. She seemed drinking his looks with hers. "I've sorter come ter think as hell's in th' hearts o' people," she went on. "There ain't no flames ez kin burn like them in people's hearts."

Roden jumped to his feet, and went over beside her. "Virginia," he said, kindly but firmly, "I'm not going to let you talk like this. Good Heaven! those country quacks know as little about medicine as I do; not as much, by Jove! for I'd not have let you leave your bed for a month yet. Come, dear, let me persuade you. Go back to bed. I'll come and see you to-morrow in your room, if your father 'll let me. You must, Virginia!"

"It ain't no worse, do you reckon," she went on, dully, "tuh be in hell than tuh have hell in you? I've thought er heap 'bout it. I've most answered it, but I'd rather—"

"Hush! hush!" said Roden, imperatively. He thought her delirious, and started to the door to call her nurse.

"Wait!" rang out her voice, with all its old, clear strength. She had risen to her feet. She was there before him. The light from the window behind her struck through her hair, so that she seemed standing between rows of living flame. "I want tuh tell you," she said. "I didn't use tuh think I was a coward, but I am—I am!" She beat the palms of her hands together, and tossed back her head as though seeking to be rid of the superflux of agony which tore her. "I kyarn' bear to say it tuh yo'; I kyarn' bear to hear yo' curse me, ez I have so often hearn yo' in my dreams. I kyarn' bear—O God!—I kyarn' bear fur yo' tuh know me ez I am. O God! O God! this 'll wipe it out, won't it? This 'll buy me peace?"

"Virginia! Virginia!" said Roden, beside himself. He tried to force her again into her chair.

"Ah! don't touch me!" she cried out—"don't yuh touch me, tuh hate me worse than ever when yuh know— Listen—listen hard, 'cause yuh ain't a-goin' to bleeve me when first yuh hear. Yuh come here tuh thank me fur savin' her life. Listen: 'twas me ez tried to kill her—'twas me! me! me!" The last word broke from her with a wild sob, almost vindictive in its urgent violence. She seemed like one who scourges mercilessly his own flesh for its sins against his soul. "I done it—I done it. I tried ter kill her. Listen! You've hearn o' fever bein' cyar'd in bits o' ribbon—in leetle bits o' velvet ribbon—one, two, ten, twenty years? There was a leetle baby died here onc't. It died o' th' fever *she* liked tuh 'a' died of. I give her that piece o' velvet to w'ar roun' her pretty throat. I went up intuh th' attic, an' hunted an' hunted till I found it in th' baby's cradle. I give it to her. I tried to kill her. O my God! Do yo' want tuh touch me—now?"

He stood and stared on her like one dazed by a sudden blow, though not quite stunned.

"You are crazy," he said, thickly. "Poor Virginia, you are crazy."

"O God!" she wailed. "I wisht I wuz— I wisht I wuz! Oh, ef I wuz only like them dumb beasts in th' stables out thar! Ef I wuz only Bonnibel, then—then—then yuh wouldn' hate me; an' ef yuh did, I wouldn' know."

"You are raving," he said again.

"Ask her—ask her, if yo' don' bleeve me. Ask her 'f Faginia Herrick didn' bring her a leetle bit o' blue velvet to w'ar round her throat the night she got wet in th' rain. She said then it smelt damp like it had been in a attic. Ask her—ask her."

"God in heaven!" said Roden, between his teeth, "can you be telling me the truth?"

"*He* knows I am!—*He* knows I am!" she said, wildly.

Roden turned from her, resting his hand on the back of the chair in which he had sat when he first entered the room. His head drooped. The double horror seemed like a palpable thing at his side.

"D' yo' bleeve me?" she said, with panting eagerness.

"Yes," he said. She would not have recognized his voice had he spoken in the dark.

She waited a few moments, motionless, frozen, as it were, with suspense and dread. Then she leaned forward, and holding fast her bosom with her crossed arms in the gesture usual with her, fixed her dilating eyes upon him. Was it possible, could it be true, that after all he could not curse her? Nay, dear God! was he even going to forgive her?

"Say somethin'," she said, in a bated voice—"say somethin'. Jess so you don' curse me, say somethin'."

Still he spoke not. She fell upon her knees and laid her head upon his feet. "O my God! my God!" she sobbed, "air yuh goin' tuh furgive me?"

Then he spoke to her. "Forgive you?" he repeated—"forgive you?" He laughed a short, rough laugh. "By G—!" he said, turning away from her, so that her forehead rested on the bare floor instead of on his feet, "it's all I can do not to curse you!"

When she rose again to her knees she was alone in the darkening room.

VIII.

Roden did not return to Caryston that night, nor the next day, nor the day after that. A boy was sent from Windemere to bring over some of his boxes. On Monday of the next week he went with the Errolls to Old Point Comfort, where Mary had been ordered to stop during her convalescence.

As much as he despised Virginia for her confession, that pathetic, joyous cry of hers as she thought him about to forgive her would sometimes ring in his ears; her deep, still, pleading look, as of some dumb beast, for mercy haunted him at times. He could feel her forehead on his feet, and the eager grasp of her hands upon them. It was not pleasant, all this; for while it annoyed and even pained him, he could not say honestly to himself that he felt any disposition to forgive her. Forgiveness is no doubt divine. Roden was quite sure that it was an attribute which, like happiness, belonged solely to the gods. As for himself, he was distinctly, vehemently, entirely human. He did not forgive — almost he did not wish to feel forgiveness. What! forgive a creature who had sought to murder his manhood's one love? Verily he would be no better than herself did he so much as dream of pardon. Between her and her God must rest that question. He would none of it. And yet why did that earnest, wistful voice, so thrilling with a timid exultation, come ever to his mental ears: "O my God! my God! air you goin' ter furgive me?" Pshaw! what balderdash! He had not cursed her. Let her comfort herself with that. He did not know many other men who would have been as forbearing. And yet again—those hands about his feet, that huddled form prone before him in humblest entreaty! It made him irritable at times. He was conscious of having acted with perfect justness, and yet he felt that his justness had not been tempered with overmuch mercy.

In the mean time Virginia lived on, if one can be said to live whose heart is dead within her. She did not dare to pray for death; she did not dare to hope for peace; she feared to die, poor ignorant child, because of the roaring flame which waited to devour her. She feared even more to live, because of the fire with which she was already consumed. She never moved save to go to bed and get up again. Sometimes she would sit all day out-of-doors under the great horse-chestnuts, already shrivelling in the June sunlight. Nothing roused her; nothing moved her in anywise. Poor old Herrick would recount to her his drollest stories, ending with a vociferous "Hyeah! hyeah!" in hopes of eliciting some answering mirth from her. But when he had reached the most excruciatingly funny climax, and paused to hear her laugh, she would turn on him her vague, gentle eyes, and say, "What's that, father?" or sometimes, "Were you a-talkin' ter me, father dear?"

The old man went heavily about his work. He was like some willing beast too late in life called upon to support a heavy burden. He was disgusted and angry to feel the big tears on his cheeks.

"The beauty of the question air," he quoth, angrily, to himself one day, "I ain't wuth th' victuals I eat. I'm a pore ole fool ez oughter be a-suckin' ov a sugar rag, 'stead o' tendin' ter er beeg place like this; but, Godamighty! ef that thar gyrl don' git a heap peerter 'fo' long, I'm gwine plumb crazy. My sakes! who'd 'a' ever thought Faginia would a-set all day like that a-studyin' her own han's like they wuz the book o' Gord! Howsomdever, 'tain't many ez studies th' book o' Gord ez faithful ez my pore leetle gyrl studies them han's o' hern. Somethin' cert'n'y *is* out o' kelter with that thar chile. Godamighty! ef Faginia wuz ter die—"

He stopped blankly in the midst of the cornfield through which he was walking, and thrusting his hands deep in his brown jeans trousers-pockets, looked up appealingly at the hot blue sky.

That same evening he was summoned as juryman to Charlottesville, a village some fifteen miles from Caryston, and as he kissed Virginia good-by his heart rose in his throat. The face she lifted to his was so wan, so patient, so like the face of her young mother just ere she died, twenty-one years ago.

"Leetle gyrl—leetle gyrl," said the old man, brokenly, "ef you don' want tuh hurry yo' father tuh his grave, yo'll hurry en take them purty leetle foots out o' yourn. Darter, honey, try 'n' git some o' them ole red roses in them white cheeks. Please, Faginia, honey, I'm 'mos' worrited to death 'long o' you."

"Pore father!" she said, stroking his face —"pore father!" that was all. Her listless hand fell again into her lap. Her eyes fixed themselves with their vague, uncomprehending look upon the far blue distance. She was as much apart from him as though she were already dead. He rose to his feet, strangling a sob in his brave old throat, that he might not distress her, and rode manfully away to his unpleasant duty.

That night a dreadful thing occurred at Caryston. The "mill stable," as it was generally called, from being built on a hill just above the mill-pond, caught on fire. There were four of Roden's most valuable horses in it, together with Bonnibel, who had been moved from the house stables while they were undergoing alteration.

Virginia was sitting silent by her bedroom window when the first copper glare began to tinge the dense upward column of black smoke. She knew in a minute what it was, although Aunt Tishy muttered something about "bresh" fires.

She leaped to her feet, her heart once more renewing its old-time measure. "Mammy!" she called—"Mammy! that's th' mill stable! th' mill stable's on fire! O God above! Th' pore horses — an' Bonnibel! O pore Mr. Jack—pore Mr. Jack! Ef Bonnibel's hurt, it'll break his heart." She had forgotten everything in her thought for him. Her own sin, his harsh words—all that had passed between them since first he gave Bonnibel into her glad keeping.

"Here!" she called, tossing on her clothes with nervous, eager fingers, "han' me my shoes—quick!—Lord God!—ef only I ken git thar in time!"

She was down-stairs and out of the house almost before the old negress knew what she was about to undertake. Out at a side gate she dashed, and down a grassy hill at the back of the house. Some catalpa-tree roots caught at her flying feet with their knotty fingers as though, fiend-like, they would hinder her on her errand of mercy. On, on; her breath came quick and laboring. She was on the open road now, straining with all her might up a steep, stone-roughed hill. All the northern heavens were ablaze with an angry orange. As she gained the top of the hill a little fan of lilac flames burst from the stable roof against the night. There was yet time—Bonnibel was in a loose-box near the door. O God, the other horses! Must they roast alive— the beautiful, agile creatures that he so loved?

Below, in the placid breast of the large pond, the lurid mass above was reflected with an effect as incongruous as when some world-tossed soul pours out its hot confession into the calm keeping of a saintly heart.

The shallow stream shoaled into fire

among the black stems of the water-reeds, and tossed the flames upon its mimic waves. She gained the rough bridge which spanned it; her feet passed with a swift, hollow sound across it. She was there — at the stable, and her breath had not yet given out. Then all at once she remembered. Oh, joy! joy! If she saved Bonnibel, and was herself hurt to death, would not that be atonement? Might he not forgive her then? Poor little savage child — poor, sweet, uncivilized, true heart! I think indeed he would forgive you if he knew.

There were men running frantically about — omnipresent — useless: they had delayed so long to set about extinguishing the fire that it was now beyond all bounds. The wild, dull trampling of the hoofs of the terrified horses made horror in the air. They whinnied and nickered like children pleading for help. One of the English grooms was dashing into the smoke and heat. Virginia seized him by the arm.

"I'm coming with you," she said; "let me keep hold of your coat."

Alas! alas! the maddened, silly brutes refused to follow. They reared madly whenever approached, and struck with their fore-feet at the plucky little lad. In no way could he approach them; threats and cajolery were in vain. Virginia snatched a whip from the stable wall and tried to beat them out. Usurper, vicious to the last, rushed furiously at her, and but for the lad's striking him over the head with a pitchfork, would inevitably have dashed her brains out with his wicked hoofs. There was no further time to be lost. One side of the roof was blazing ominously, and the wall on the eastern side began to tremble.

Virginia, in spite of entreaties and hands held out to stop her, turned her skirts about her head and went into Bonnibel's box. "Six of us 'ave tried to get 'er out, miss," said the panting lad, who had followed her. "Don't you venture in, for God's sake, miss;

she's that mad she'll kill you — th' poor hussy!"

Bonnibel was in truth like a horse distraught. She was leaping back and forth, and trotting from side to side of her capacious box, nickering from time to time, with head aloft and tail held like a plume above her satin quarters. No sooner did she hear Virginia's voice than she stopped short, quivering in every splendid limb and sinew.

"Bonnibel!" said Virginia, in that soft monotone the frightened creature had not now heard for many a day — "Bonnibel!" There was a second's pause; then stooping her bright head, with a low whinny as of welcome and trust, the gallant mare came to the well-known voice.

Virginia tore off her woollen shawl and blindfolded the bright eyes.

In the mean time the rest of the English lads and the head groom had arrived, with fire-engines and more help. They had already succeeded in getting the horse out. The vicious Usurper they were compelled to leave to his awful fate.

"Boys, Bonnibel's coming!" yelled the lad who had entered the stable with Virginia, dashing out ahead of her; "Miss Herrick's got her, and she's coming kind as a lamb!"

A hearty, roaring cheer went up from without, mingled with exultant warwhoops from the negroes gathered around.

Almost they were safe. Why do things happen with only an inch between safety and destruction? One instant more and horse and woman would have been free. But in that tarrying instant a heavy beam from the front of the stable fell crashing down, bringing with it a great mass of bricks and mortar. Virginia and Bonnibel were half buried under the reeking mass. The flames sent up an exultant roar as of triumph. There was a smothered, horrified groan from the men, and then

Bonnibel, freeing herself by one powerful effort of her iron quarters, galloped off into the coolness of the night.

They pulled Virginia out, with such gentleness as they could spare to the encroaching flames, and a bed was instantly made for her on the damp turf by means of the men's hastily torn-off coats. She lay there, still, white, most beautiful, with peace at last upon her tired face. Did she dream, perchance, that he forgave her?

Ah! but the horror that followed—the crash succeeding crash, the hideous rioting of the vengeful flames about the poor brutes within. Some were suffocated, some jammed to death beneath the continually falling masses of stone and brick. Usurper, dauntless, rebellious to the last, struck with his iron-shod feet at the flames that made too free with him. He was so magnificent in his fierce disdain that more than one of the grooms sobbed like girls at the fate which had overtaken him. All at once a cry, piercing, shrill, terrible above any sound which had ever come upon their hearing, shook the stillness of the night to shuddering echoes. It was the one and only sign of pain that Usurper gave ere he sank to an awful death among the blazing ruins.

Virginia's senses returned to her as they were carrying her home in solemn silence and with bared heads. She tried to lift herself on one elbow, and sank back with a moan of pain; but even for that there went up some muttered thanks from the men who carried her. They had thought her dead.

"Does the moving pain you, miss?" asked the lad who had been with her in Bonnibel's box.

"It hurts some," she said, bravely. "What's happened?"

They had to tell her all about the fire, as though it were a thing new to her, and how she had saved Bonnibel.

"Oh, did I?" she said. "Did I?—air yuh sure?"

"Sure, miss?" echoed the admiring Hicks. "Sure? Well, I think we be pretty sure o' that 'ere! Bean't we, boys?"

They could not say enough.

One thought was making music in Virginia's heart. "Perhaps he'll forgive me now," she said over and over to herself. She looked upward at the starry heavens through the broad leaves of the catalpa-trees, as they bore her up the last hill to the house, with a feeling closely akin to joy. "I've saved Bonnibel," she thought— "I've saved Bonnibel, anyways; ef he don't forgive me, I've done somethin' to make him glad. 'Twas awful in that burnin' place; but I saved her—I saved her—I saved her." She said the last three words out loud.

"That you did, miss," said the boy Hicks, who walked close beside her. "Tell her again, boys."

They told her over and over again, first one and then the other; she seemed never tired of listening. For the first time in many, many days her white lips fell into the gracious curves they used to know so well. She was smiling—smiling for sheer happiness. She was hurt to death, she knew that; something whispered it in her glad ears as distinctly as though the good God had bent from his great heavens himself to tell her so; and she knew—ah! she knew — that her God had forgiven her. Death had brought her two gifts so sweet in his chill arms that his embrace scarcely frightened her. As they carried her with slow carefulness up the front steps and into the wide hall an innocent fancy seized her; she would like so much to die in Mr. Jack's room—on his little iron bed. There couldn't be any harm, could there? She looked so wistfully up into the face of little Hicks that he felt she wanted something, and asked her what it was.

"Kyar me into Mr. Jack's room," she whispered. "It's—it's nearer the ground."

The pretty subterfuge was also a very good one. It would have been almost mortal anguish to her, had they sought to bear her poor wrecked body up that winding stair-way.

So into "Mr. Jack's room" they carried her, and placed her full gently on his forsaken bed.

Aunt Tishy came hurrying with inarticulate cries. They hushed her as best they might, telling her that any disturbance might kill the girl. Then little Hicks mounted one of Roden's best horses and dashed off in search of a surgeon.

Virginia lay quiet and quite content, staring with wide-open eyes at the well-known objects in the airy room. Another delightful fancy seized upon her. Ah! it was good to lie there and die, and pretend that she had been his wife, and that it was her right to die in there with all those much-loved manly kickshaws about her: the Scotch deer-stalker's cap, which hung on one of the sconces of a little mirror over the mantle; that heap of glittering spurs on a table near at hand; his whip; his boots; an old blue flannel shirt on the bed's foot. She had not allowed any one to enter his room since he left for Windemere, nor had she herself been in it.

And even if he didn't forgive her, she saved Bonnibel. Suddenly there came upon her an awful, crashing agony.

"Mammy! mammy!" she called, in her childhood's voice. She clung to her old nurse with might and main. "Oh, mammy, mammy, I'm payin' fur it! Yuh don' know, but I'm payin' fur it. I'm so glad—I'm so glad! Mammy, sing me 'bout 'though yo' sins be as scarlet'—sing! sing!"

The old negress, as well as she could for sobbing, sang to her in such words as these:

"'Tis de old ship o' Zion,
   Come to take us all ho-ome—
   Glory, glory, hallelujah!
'Tis de old ship o' Zion,

> Come to take us all home—
> Glory, glory, hallelujah!"

Here she broke off with a pitiful cry: "O Gord! my sweet lamb, mammy kyarn' sing to you while her heart's fyar breakin' in her. Don' ask pore mammy tuh sing, my honey—don', don'!"

"Sing, please, sing," said the girl, with gentle insistence. Her mind was failing her a little for the first time. "God alluz furgives, don' he, mammy? Alluz, alluz. Sing 'bout it, mammy; please, mammy, sing."

The old negress went on, brokenly:

> "We has landed many thousands—
> Hallelujah!
> An' we'll lan' many mo-re—
> Hallelujah!"

"Please sing 'bout the sins, mammy; that's what I want—'bout the sins."

The poor old woman crooned on, swaying her body to and fro as she crouched at the bedside:

"Do' yo' sins be as skyarlet,
  Dey shall be as white as snow—
  Glory, glory, hallelujah!
Do' yo' sins be as skyarlet,
  Dey shall be as white as snow—
  Glory, glory, hallelujah!
'Tis Jesus is deir Capt'in—
  Hallelujah!
'Tis Jesus is deir Capt'in—
  Hallelujah!"

"White ez snow—white ez snow," murmured the girl. "Mammy, do yo' bleeve that? Ain't it sweet, mammy? don' it seem good an' kind? Mammy, yo' see that ole blue shirt a-hangin' thar? I loves that shirt, mammy, same as some women loves their children. It's sorter got his shape now, ain't it? Hand it here, mammy. Don' it smell good?—kinder briery an' soapy, mammy? He used to take more barths 'n any man yo' ever hearn ov. I used ter hear him a-splashin' clear up in my room. Where's father, mammy? I do want to see father, an' I want to see Bonnibel 'fore I go. She came to me—oh, so sweet an' lovin'! She knew I'd 'a' died fur her, I reckon. Mammy, did yo' sen' fur father? Pore father! pore father! he'll be so sorry! Oh, pore father!" Here the first tears she had shed rolled over her white cheeks. The old negress sobbed out aloud.

"Oh, my honey!" she said—"oh, my little lamb!—oh, my honey!"

Again came that terrible pain, almost beyond her power to endure.

"I'm payin' fur it—I'm payin' fur it," she said, over and over again. "God's so good to me! He's forgiven me; he's lettin' me pay fur it."

The surgeon came at daybreak. He was quiet and serious. Little Hicks was the only one to whom he told anything. To him he said, "She may live two or three days; she may die before night."

At one o'clock next day old Herrick returned. He was wordless and almost majestic in his deep grief. All day long he sat holding her in such positions as would ease her; talking to her; trying to follow her wandering fancies. She knew him always, though she knew no one else. "Father," she said, suddenly, in one of the intervals when reason returned to her, "won't you please sen' fur Mr. Jack? Somethin' in my heart tells me he'll come —now. Write to him 'bout Bonnibel. Tell him I saved her. Tell him I jess want ter say good-by. I don' wan' him ever ter furgive me. I only want to—to look at him once more. Father "—wistfully—"*you* think he'll come?"

"Yes, yes, my little girl, I think he'll come."

"Then write, write, father—quick. Don' let it be too late. I wan' so bad to look at him once more!"

He came—oh yes, he came! mad with regret and remorse, repentant, eager to atone. "Where is she? where is she?"

he asked as he threw down his hat upon the hall table, and jerked off his spurs, that their jingling might not disturb her. If he had only known the music that they made to her ears!

"She's in yo' room, sur. They tells me ez how 'twar her fancy to be took thar," said Herrick, simply. "I hope ez you don' min', sur."

Mind! Jack's eyes were hot with the saddest tears of all his life.

He went in softly. There she lay, pathetic, fragile as some long-ill child upon his narrow bed. He went and stooped over her, taking into one of his brown hands her restless, slender fingers. Her gentle look rested unknowingly upon him.

"Ain't they goin' ter sen' fur Mr. Jack?" she said. "I think he'll come—now; father thought ez how he would. Please write it down that I saved Bonnibel—please write that down. 'Twas mighty hot, but I saved her. Oh, don' yo' think he'll come?—don' yo' think he'll come? I don' even arst him to speak to me. Ef he'll only stand in th' door so ez I kin see him when I go."

"Virginia—Virginia," said Roden, brokenly. "My dear little girl, don't you know me? Here I am!—here—at your side. Don't you feel my hands, Virginia? Don't you know me?"

She went rambling on. "I wonder ef he would furgive me ef he knew? I wisht Bonnibel could tell him—I wisht I was Bonnibel!" with a little rippling laugh infinitely pathetic. "Oh, wouldn' I kyar him pretty an' straight at his fences, an' win ev'y race fur him!" Her eyes opened vague and sorrowful again upon Roden's pale face. "Oh," she said, with a long sighing breath, "don't you think he'll come? Write to him 'bout Bonnibel—please write that ter him."

"Virginia, look at me—look at me," said the young man, half lifting her in his arms.

"Dear little Virginia, here I am. I forgive you with all my heart and soul, Virginia. Oh, please look at me, please remember me."

"Who says 'furgive?'" she said, with her restless, eager eyes searching the room as if for something long expected—"who says 'furgive?'"

"I do, I do," Roden said, weeping at last like any girl. "I forgive you, Virginia— Virginia. You *shall* know me!"

Her eyes fixed themselves upon his face, first vacantly, then with a wonder-stricken radiance. "Mr. Jack," she said, under her breath, "did they tell yo'? I saved her; that's all. Yo' needn' say nothin'; I jess wanted to look at yo'. I saved her. 'Twas awful hot. I kin hear it roarin' now. She come to me; she wouldn' come to nobody else."

"Virginia," said Roden, "listen to me; stop talking. What do I care about Bonnibel? Child, do you want to break my heart? Listen, Virginia; I forgive you—I *forgive you.*"

"Do—you—really?" she said, with the old timid joy in her soft voice. "I ain't dreamin'? Well, God's so good to me! But I did save her. 'Bonnibel!' I said—'Bonnibel!' an' she come right straight ter me with her pretty head tucked down. Then came all that fire on us. I thought 'twas over. But I saved her—I saved her. Please tell him that—*please* tell him that. I reckon he'll sorter remember me kind fur that; don' you, father?"

After a while her reason came again. She asked to see Bonnibel; they could bring her to the window, she said, and she would like also to give her a handful of grass.

They rolled the bed to the window, and little Hicks led Bonnibel up beside it. Roden went out himself and gathered a handful of fresh grass. I think the lad only respected his master more for the tears that ran down his cheeks. He couldn't see very distinctly himself just then, this good little Hicks.

"Bonnibel," said the girl, in her cooing tones—"Bonnibel."

What was the matter? Had suffering charged some magic in that soft voice? Bonnibel turned indifferently away from the anxious hand, and rubbed her bright head with an impatient movement against one of her fore-legs.

"Oh!" said the girl, while the glad flush died out of her face, and the green blades fell from her hold upon the window-sill, "Bonnibel don' know me any more—she don' care. I gave my life for her, an'—an' she don' care."

"Yes, she does—she does," said Roden, frantic for her disappointment; "she's just gorged, the little glutton! She's been out at grass ever since you saved her, Virginia dear; that's all."

"No, 'tain't," said the girl, sadly. "I

ain't the same, I reckon; I reckon I'm right near gone, Mr. Jack. Well, I saved her, anyhow. The most part fell on me; she kicked herself loose. Please, father, ef Mr. Jack don' come in time—*please*, father, tell him ez how I saved Bonnibel. Oh, father, I mus' tell somebody 'fore I go. I kyarn' bear to think there won't be anybody in all th' world ez knows it when I'm gone. I loved him, father dear—I loved him so! An' I've been mighty wicked; an' God's been mighty good ter me; an' I'm goin' to heaven, mammy says. But I won't have him even there—I won't have him—even there."

The soft voice broke suddenly—stopped. The bright head dropped forward on her breast.

Roden had buried his face in her two pale hands. When he looked up, old Herrick was closing gently with his toil-roughened hand the sweet wide eyes which never more would look on anything this side the stars.

It was at this moment that Bonnibel, repenting, perhaps, of her former coldness, thrust in her little deer-head at the open window, and drew a long sighing breath as of contentment.

The blades of grass dropped from the thin hand now so still upon the stirless bosom were blown along the window-sill by the mare's warm breath.

THE END.

A BROTHER TO DRAGONS,
AND OTHER OLD-TIME TALES.

By AMÉLIE RIVES.   Post 8vo, Cloth, Extra, $1 00.

Not alone in the success in reproducing the antique diction are they remarkable, but in getting the color and atmosphere of the period. . . . In the observation of natural objects, and above all the knowledge of the human heart, is found the promise that this work holds forth. . . . The volume takes high rank in the department which marks the most notable achievements of American letters at the present day.—*N. Y. Commercial Advertiser.*

How well Miss Rives has sustained and added to the reputation she so suddenly won, we all know, and the permanency of that reputation demonstrates conclusively that her success did not depend upon the lucky striking of a popular fancy, but that it rests upon enduring qualities that are developing more and more richly year by year.—*Richmond State.*

Miss Rives is a woman of most undoubted power. She has imagination, daring, and an exquisite sense of form.—*N. Y. Star.*

Three of Miss Amélie Rives's most brilliant stories. . . . Their quaint old-time manner gives them a peculiar charm.—*Philadelphia Bulletin.*

Three striking stories of very unusual force and fertility of thought and diction and strong dramatic feeling, added to which is a quick and sympathetic fancy.—*N. Y. Sun.*

Here is pathos which is not morbid ; and though the humor is broad, it is in perfect keeping with the time and the characters of the supposed narrators. These three stories are rich in promise.—*Critic*, N. Y.

For more reasons than one Miss Rives is seen at her best in old-time tales such as she shows us in this volume. The atmosphere with which these tales are clothed is especially congenial to her, and she can work within its influence with remarkable success.—*Brooklyn Times.*

It is evident that the author has imagination in an unusual degree, much strength of expression, and skill in delineating character.—*Boston Journal.*

There are few young writers who begin a promising career with so much spontaneity and charm of expression as is displayed by Miss Rives in this volume.—*Literary World*, Boston.

PUBLISHED BY HARPER & BROTHERS, NEW YORK.

☞ HARPER & BROTHERS *will send the above work by mail, postage prepaid, to any part of the United States or Canada, on receipt of the price.*

CAPTAIN MACDONALD'S DAUGHTER.

A Novel. By ARCHIBALD CAMPBELL. 16mo, Cloth, Extra, $1 00.

It is a genuinely pathetic tale, and shows a keen and accurate knowledge of human nature under many varying conditions.—*Saturday Evening Gazette*, Boston.

A story of sound moral quality and touching pathos.—*N. Y. Commercial Advertiser.*

There are many excellent delineations of scenes and life in Scotland, Virginia, and Florida. . . . The characters are also carefully studied and successfully drawn. The heroine, the warm-hearted, impulsive, and gifted Nan, especially, is a very charming personage. . . . As a quiet story, with a pathetic vein running through it, we can confidently recommend it to all.—*Congregationalist*, Boston.

Full of life and movement, and marked by both power and pathos.—*Zion's Herald*, Boston.

The characters are very well drawn, and there is a natural development of the plot. . . . The descriptions of scenery are vivid and life-like, and the scenes are totally free from the extravagance which mars so much contemporary fiction. The author of this work will be heard from again.—*Christian Intelligencer*, N. Y.

A novel of Scottish life, shifting to American scenes, and gives the reader a glimpse of life in Virginia and Florida. The story is told with much simplicity, though a study of heredity is inwrought with the artless narrative. . . . The story is quiet in action, but will please lovers of naturalness and faithful character delineation.—*Commonwealth*, Boston.

The characters of the story are strong and the book well written.—*Christian Advocate*, N. Y.

A strong hand has drawn the minister's household in the manse of Strathlowrie. Surely the author must have at some time made one of just such a Scotch family, so graphic are the touches of reality. . . . Seldom has a grave story of a minister's household been told with such a rippling accompaniment of humor.—*Philadelphia Ledger.*

A bright, engaging book, sparkling with shrewd Scotch wit on nearly every page, and ends most satisfactorily.—*Christian at Work*, N. Y.

PUBLISHED BY HARPER & BROTHERS, NEW YORK.

☞ HARPER & BROTHERS *will send the above work by mail, postage prepaid, to any part of the United States or Canada, on receipt of the price.*

www.ingramcontent.com/pod-product-compliance
Lightning Source LLC
Chambersburg PA
CBHW021827230426
43669CB00008B/889